They Call Him John Q.
A Hotel Legend

Susan M. Drake

PANTS
PUBLISHING

Published by Black Pants Publishing, LLC
34510 S. Tournament Drive
Memphis, TN 38125

Cover design and typography: Colleen Wells

Publisher's Cataloging-in-Publication
(Provided by Quality books, Inc.)

Drake, Susan M.
    They call him John Q. : a hotel legend / by Susan M.
Drake
    p. cm.
    LCCN: 2002110613
    ISBN: 0970373651 (pbk.)
    ISBN: 0970373600 (hardcover)

    1. Hammons, John Q. 2. Hotelkeepers–United States–
Biography. 3. Hospitality industry–United States–
Biography. 1. Title.

TX910.5.H28D73 2002   338.7'616479473'0092
                           QBI02-200615

This book is printed on acid-free paper.

They Call Him John Q.
Table of Contents

Acknowledgments

You will know people by the friends they keep, and John Q. has some amazingly special friends. In 83 years, he has met a mighty lot of people, some high profile, some less so; friends and business partners, allies, casual acquaintances and strangers. It would be impossible to include all 83 years' worth of those people, or to even vaguely describe what they have contributed to this book. We are hopeful that we've included a broad enough range to give a glimpse of who John Q. is and what makes him the legend he has become.

There are a few people to whom I would like to offer special thanks. First, there is Susan Steinbrecher, who introduced me to this project, and Lou Weckstein and Scott Tarwater whose goal was to make this book about their Chairman a reality. I am forever indebted for the chance to record the life of an icon. When they asked me to do this project, I knew that John Q. was a special person; I had no idea just how special. Through the project I have grown to admire and respect him, to appreciate his humor and to understand what a mighty person he is. I am deeply honored to have been given this responsibility.

I also appreciate the sanction and help of Jan Robbins, Cheryl McGee and Marty McGahan, who provided immeasurable help and generously added their own glorious sense of humor and friendship. And thank you to all of the John Q. Hammons associates who generously took the time to tell me of their own experiences with John Q. Above all, nothing would have been possible without Susan Gross, whose editing and other contributions are beyond value.

I have done little except record the memories and insights of the people who shared with me their stories of this man. They essentially "colored" the book, expressing the personality that is John Q. Hammons.

And finally, to John Q. Hammons, I give my thanks. He has inspired so many people. I count myself among those who are better for having known him.

To our Founder and Chairman:

Thank you. We know you frequently hear those words from civic leaders after investing $30 or $40 million in a local economy. But how often do your associates take the time to say *thank you* for providing us the opportunity to be an integral part of the incredible hotel machine that has earned a reputation for being the "best of the best" throughout the hospitality world?

You call upon your decades of experience for continued growth and expansion, but if you add up the years of service we also bring to the company, the combined total quickly becomes centuries. That's how much your associates care for John Q. Hammons Hotels — that's how dedicated we are to our Founder and Chairman.

Do you remember what you said when you hired many of us? That you expect three things — honesty, loyalty and hard work. Well, we're over 10,000 strong now and represent a formidable force of honest, loyal and hard-working people — just like our Founder.

While many entrepreneurs talk the talk, you not only walk the walk but you've been on a dead run for over 80 years. You've got the late night phone calls down to a science - both west and east coasts. No matter what the hour, you're always checking the hotels to see if they're full, if all the systems are working, or how long the person answering the phone has worked there. Many associates have met you in person when you've visited their hotel; some immediately recognize your voice when you call a hotel looking for the general manager or director of sales; and some of us work with you on a daily basis. It makes no matter . . . you're always the same. You're the man, the myth, and the legend. You've taught us that quality and value sell, and we all work hard everyday to ensure that happens.

Your influence on our country's young children may not become evident within your lifetime, but understand that your investments in education and the arts will pay dividends for generations to come. Once a teacher, always a teacher. But you've coupled your teaching talents with entrepreneurial savvy and more drive than most. The things many of us have learned in our years of service on your team could never have been gleaned from a classroom setting. As written by Andy Rooney, a man who has the gift of saying so much with very few words, "I've learned . . . that the best classroom in the world is at the feet of an elderly person." And while no one who knows you thinks of you as elderly, your wisdom knows no end. We appreciate our autonomy; we applaud the opportunities afforded us.

What type of leader is it that inspires people to want to work well into the night or arrive many hours before dawn to meet deadlines? We continue to work side by side to bring your visions to reality — to help make your dreams come true. Your vision quietly becomes our vision, and while we may not always understand or even agree with your methods, rest assured we all continue to devote 110% of our talent and effort to see that the company's goals are achieved.

While you may be legendary throughout the hospitality world and even to many of our own associates who have yet to meet you, you'll always be the country boy from Fairview, Missouri, where you're still known as Quentin. Your best times are spent sharing stories about your childhood, about the tough and lasting life lessons you've learned, about your parents, about lifelong friends and mentors. We appreciate hearing about those times, and we appreciate your interest in our personal lives.

In 1999, every person in the corporate office participated in a

Thanksgiving tribute by writing a nice word or sentiment about each of his or her co-workers. The list describing you and your life contained words and phrases like "visionary; teacher and leader; legend; powerful; distinguished and inspiring; a paternal soul (whether he admits it or not)." And while you could never quite grasp the premise behind this whole endeavor, you've often asked to read "the list" just one more time. It's a good thing we saved it for you!

We know that you're more likely to become nervous over a meeting with a young terminally ill child than you are walking into a boardroom full of city officials. The city part represents your business; the time spent lending support and inspiration to a child represents your humanity. You are gracious in both arenas.

Many of us have witnessed your tears as you reflect back to the Great Depression and how it affected your mother and father. Thank you for trusting us with your emotional frailties; we value your humanness.

Do we admire your tenacity? Yes, most of the time. It's the very force that continually reminds us that we do have what it takes to meet the next challenge. We appreciate your choice of leaders to take our company to new heights; we applaud your willingness to empower those leaders who are tasked with making the difficult choices which face not only our industry but also the host of issues which impact our country and ultimately everyone's personal lives. We share in your admiration and love of our great nation, the United States of America.

Whether you recognize it or not, Mr. Hammons, you have a rare gift. It's your uncanny ability to motivate people at all levels who are willing to do what it takes to bring a project in on time; to close a deal against all odds; to overcome seemingly insurmountable bureaucratic obstacles in order to complete a task. How do you do it? Is it because you exhibit the same three principles you

demand of those around you? Honesty, loyalty and hard work?
We would all like to think so.

We're protective of you and your reputation. And while we may
battle with you in the morning, we'd be the first to rise to your
defense should anyone attempt to impugn your name.

We salute our Founder and Chairman — a visionary and legend.
You're our leader and friend. Thank you for the opportunities
you've afforded us so that our personal dreams may come true.
We're proud of you, and we stand united beside you.

Your Officers, Staff, Associates and
Friends of John Q. Hammons Hotels

1

If He Builds It, They Will Come

In 1974, John Q. Hammons paid a Jeep driver $25 to take him to the top of a mountain on Table Rock Lake in the Ozarks. Atop that mountain, Hammons was convinced, he would build a hotel one day. No matter that he would have to blast 50 feet off the mountain to flatten it enough to build the hotel. No matter that it was far from any major highway, without much chance of drop-in traffic. No matter that the closest civilization, Branson, Missouri, was just a two-lane town with a few entertainers. No matter that it would cost $60 million and take almost two years to build the hotel. When John Q. has a vision, nothing stands in his way. He bought the property, held onto it for 26 years and when he believed the time was right, he made his move.

Today, you don't need a Jeep to get to the top of the mountain. Pass through Branson, and you'll encounter a $1.7 billion tourist mecca, the number one motorcoach destination of the decade. Go south, cruise around Table Rock Lake and you'll see a clear path to The Chateau on the Lake, a 301-room European-style hotel complete with a 46-foot tall, $85,000 tree "growing" up from its lobby. Nearby, a multistory waterfall and rock display is home to woodland creatures. Visit the movie theater, or rent a boat or take a shuttle to the Branson attractions. Tour the 40,000-square-foot meeting facilities (as big as a football field), and you'll see $75,000 worth of murals of castles on the walls.

Check in and don't be surprised if you see a celebrity. Baseball legend Stan Musial has stayed there with his family. And John Q. loves to tell the story of when Walter Cronkite visited the hotel. He asked Cronkite what he thought of the property. "He told me, 'I can't believe this hotel; I've been all over the world and it ranks at the top.'" Perhaps Cronkite stayed in the presidential suite, with its $3,000 showerhead. Even the regular guest rooms have Brazilian granite and Italian marble in the bathrooms.

This is The Chateau, John Q. Hammons' vision come true. On his game of Monopoly, it's Park Place and Boardwalk all rolled into one. Branson leaders called The Chateau a "jewel," a "mountaintop beacon for a new market of visitors: upscale conventioneers and vacationers."

BEING A VISIONARY IS WHAT JOHN Q. IS ALL ABOUT. HE'S NOT ABOUT WHAT IS, HE'S ABOUT WHAT MIGHT BE.

So what's this? An advertisement for John Q. Hammons' hotels? Not at all: It's his life. You see, you can't talk about John Q. without talking about his hotels, the big, beautiful properties that have adorned cities in 40 states throughout his career.

John Q.'s Crystal Ball

Being a visionary is what John Q. is all about. He's not about what *is*; he's about what *might be.* And he's pretty upfront about his talent for seeing the future: "I was way ahead of the boom in Branson," he says.

Indeed, at the time John Q. first invested his imagination in Branson, its potential was something only a few people could see, and even fewer would put their money where their imaginations were. But John Q. isn't shy about "placing bets." He's bet on a lot of locations from which others would shy away. In the case of The Chateau, it was a $60 million one. That's a big stake for a hotel that's not within an hour of an airport, and even further from a major city. Some still think it may not be a wise business decision, but John Q. would argue that. Five years after its opening, the hotel's business is growing steadily. It's not the first venture he's pursued that others couldn't imagine. Not by a long shot. Somehow, some way, John Q. can make impossible deals happen, can just about always get money when no one else can and will literally move mountains to create a successful hotel.

That's because he knows what's over the hill…and it sure isn't John Q.

"People do not stop to think what change means," says John Q. "That's the thing about success. You have to watch change in people, change in habits, change in style, change in desire, change in everything. It's happening every day, and nobody thinks about it. I do."

A lot of what changes in John Q.'s world is a direct result of him changing it.

"It's not the making of money that interests me so much as the creation of projects and keeping abreast of what's happening in the world each day," he says.

Considering his age—83—some people—those who don't know him well—might laugh when he says he's looking to get a $35- or $45-million loan with a long-term payback. Jim Anderson, president of the Springfield, Missouri, Chamber of Commerce, says it's really no obstacle. "When bankers find out who he is, age doesn't matter. A few years ago, a mayor in another community told me, 'This guy is 81, looks 60, and acts 40.'"

Two years after that comment was made, John Q. still looks 60 and acts 40. And just like back when he began, there's no stopping John Q. "Most people would worry about borrowing $100,000. He doesn't worry about borrowing $100 million!" says Tom Harwell, Hammons' regional vice president. But then, John Q. is not most people. He's used to doing things in a bigger, better way than the rest of the world. When he makes a mark, it's an exclamation point.

HE HAS SINGLE-HANDEDLY, AS A ONE-MAN BAND, BUILT MORE HOTELS—THAT IS, QUALITY HOTELS—THAN ANYONE IN AMERICA.

Basketball coach Barry Hinson, SMSU, jokes, "When John Q. Hammons dies, he will go up to heaven and St. Peter will meet him at the gate. Above the gate will be a large sign that says, 'Welcome to Heaven, a John Q. Hammons Development.'"

Who Is John Q. Hammons?

John Q., as everyone calls him, is one of the premier hotel developers in the United States. His name may not be as instantly recognizable to the public as those of some of the other legends of the hospitality industry, like Kemmons Wilson, who founded Holiday Inn, or Bill Marriott or Conrad Hilton. But while those legends were busy making a name for themselves, John Q. was busy building hotels. Lots of hotels. It made him an icon in the hotel industry.

"I'll bet when he was 30 years old, he couldn't have bought a hamburger," says Mickey Powell, a franchise director with Hilton Hotels. " But he put it all together."

He put it together all right. "He has single-handedly, as a one-man band, built more hotels—that is, quality hotels—than anyone in America," says Michael D. Rose, chairman of Gaylord Entertainment and former chairman of Promus Hotels. In fact, over the course of his 40-plus-year career, Hammons has built some 145 hotels in 40 states. His public company now owns or manages 56 hotels, and is considered to be the leading independent builder and manager of hotel meeting space in the country, with more than 1.7 million square feet of meeting and convention space. He personally owns about 77 percent of the public company John Q. Hammons Hotels, Inc., is a partner in Winegardner and Hammons, Inc., that owns and manages hotels, and he has a private company through which he invests in projects when the spirit moves him…which it constantly does. All told, his companies are responsible for three million square feet of meeting and convention space.

One of his annual reports boasts, "Building on the Past, Developing for the Future," and that statement speaks to his fanatic commitment to quality and creating something with long-lasting value. The hotel brands he builds and operates are like a list of who's who in the industry: Embassy Suites, Marriott, Homewood Suites by Hilton, Hampton Inn & Suites, Holiday Inn, Sheraton, Renaissance, Residence Inn by Marriott and Courtyard by Marriott. John Q. even has his own signature atrium brand, Plaza Hotels.

When he gets ready to open a hotel, he announces it with a simple but definitive statement: "Another Exceptional Hotel by John Q. Hammons." And nobody's arguing that point. Every year his hotels take home awards—sometimes multiple awards—from the franchise companies he's associated with. He's been in *Forbes* magazine and has rubbed shoulders with the former British Prime Minister Margaret Thatcher, Wal-Mart founder Sam Walton, and former Presidents Jimmy Carter and George Bush. He owns a large portion of Springfield, Missouri, population 300,000, and his charitable contributions in that city alone top $50 million. At a dinner in 1985, comedian Bob Hope said, "It won't be long before this town is called Hammonsville, Missouri."

The public hotel company has revenues of about $450 million. But hotels aren't the only thing in John Q.'s life. He's involved in about 80 companies across the country, in lines of business ranging from business journal publishing to fast food to catering. Besides hotels, he has developed IMAX theaters, a riverboat casino in Joliet, Illinois, and rental storage facilities in California and Missouri, to name a few of his diverse investments. Aside from his own money-making projects, he's also a key contributor to non-profit groups that benefit the performing arts, education, sports and children. His total business worth? Since not all of his companies are public, that's a good question. Suffice it to say, it's a lot.

Believe it or not, that's actually a very short list of his accomplishments. But who is John Q. Hammons?

"He is without doubt a dreamer and a visionary, a riverboat gambler who's not afraid to bluff," says Joe Morrissey, regional vice president of the John Q. Hammons Midwest region.

Not Everybody Knows His Name

At one point, John Q. let his driver's license expire (he discovered it on a business trip when he tried to rent a car). His friend Mickey Powell—whom he refers to as "Mayor"—was involved in getting the new license.

"He said, 'My God, Mayor, my driver's license has expired!' I said, well, I just got mine last week, and I had to take a test. He said, 'I'm not going to take a test. I'll get Jan (his assistant) to call the state police and tell them to send me one over.'"

Jan called, and the director of the license bureau said that they wouldn't make him take a test, but they did require that he come in, fill out the information and have his picture taken. Mickey accompanied him.

"This young clerical girl, about 20 years old, is typing out the form. She was asking him a lot of standard questions. 'What's your name? What's your age? What's your home address?' Suddenly, Hammons stopped short. 'I don't know my street address! Mayor, what's my street address?' Of course I didn't know, so he said, 'Honey, it's in Southern Hills.' And she said, 'I need your street address.' So I'm looking up his street address in the phone book, and she asks the next question: 'What's your occupation?' So he gave kind of a little laugh, and he said, 'Well, I don't know. Mayor, what would you say I do for a living?' The little girl said, 'What do you do?' And he said, 'Well, honey, I'm John Q. Hammons, you know me; you know who I am.' And she said, 'Well, no sir, Mr. Hammons, I don't know who you are, but if you're unemployed, you just need to go ahead and tell me so right now.'"

Risk-taker, Philosopher, Philanthropist

He's definitely not unemployed. Never has been. Wouldn't know how. He's a man who has earned millions, a man who has walked with legends, a man who has employed many and enlightened more. He's famous, and he's rich. But most importantly, he's a man you'll enjoy getting to know.

Tom Keltner, executive vice president of Hilton Hotels Corporation says, "I don't always agree with John, but I always feel glad I had the conversation."

John Q. Words of Wisdom

*Circulated at the request of John Q. Hammons

A Golden Rule for Success

"I want to take the calculated risk, to dream and to build, to fail and to succeed, to turn my back on security in search of opportunity, and never be numbered with those weak and timid souls who have known neither victory or defeat."

Author Unknown

2

The Rabbit Trap

The theme of the enormously popular Survivor TV series is "Outwit, Outplay, Outlast." It could be the theme for John Q. Hammons, a man who, in his industry, has done all three. He surely could survive on a deserted island, in the Outback or in any type of jungle, and he would probably turn it into a profit-making tourist destination. All he would need is one other person there to make a deal with.

Growing up in Fairview, Missouri, was no picnic for James Quentin Hammons. Born February 24, 1919, to James O. and Hortense Bass Hammons, he was just 10 years old when the U. S. stock market crashed, ultimately losing a third of its value. Like millions of American families, John's was hard hit.

The son of a dairy farmer, Quentin, as he was known, always did what he could to help out. "As hard as it was, I had to work. They trained me to work from day one. All summer long I'd get on a thrasher run. I did everything to make money. They paid me 50 cents a day."

Winter in Missouri was harsh. "There was an orchard next to our farm, and in the wintertime they had this old tall sage grass. For a little boy, you couldn't hardly see over the top. That was an excellent place for hunting." At 12 years old, Quentin would brave the cold to set 20 or so rabbit traps. "I would make the traps out of old wood, because if you made them out of new wood, the rabbits wouldn't go in. I'd bait it with an apple or a turnip," he says. "I was averaging five to six pelts a day, and I sold them for five cents apiece. So I was getting rich."

One day, however, when he arrived at his customary 6 a.m. to collect his rabbits, there were none. The next day none, three days in a row. Finally, a neighbor told Hammons' father that a boy who lived nearby was arriving before Quentin and stealing his catch. "It was a 16-year-old, bully-type kid," says Hammons. "That kid was a thief." Quentin's way of solving the problem was to work around it. The next morning he got up earlier. He arrived at the traps about 4 a.m. "I had four rabbits the first morning, so I beat the thief. That's a true story."

He's been getting up earlier ever since.

The rabbit story has become so much a part of the personal history that shaped his life, his friend, Dr. Marshall Gordon, gave him a replica of a rough-hewn rabbit trap; it's enshrined in the John Q. Hammons Library, just one of the thousands of memorable events in a life that spans 83 years. Not only does it stand for his own chin-up attitude about making it on your own, it also reminds everyone that with John Q., honesty is the best policy for a very good reason.

Despite his efforts and his family's determination, the Great

---

"I SWORE I WOULD NEVER BE POOR."

Depression took its toll. "My parents lost the farm. I stood in the field and watched my father cry. That was a profound moment in my life," says John Q. "My mother had to go to work in a tomato factory. She was not in good health, and that really made an impression on me, going down there and seeing her working. She wasn't really able to work as much as she had to, I didn't think. That affected me. Not the fact that she had to work like that—she worked hard at home—but the fact that she really wasn't well. For her to leave home and do that; that was a new world for me. I swore I would never be poor."

Getting Bitten by the Sports Bug

After they lost the farm, John's father went to work selling insurance, and John went on to Fairview High School. There he found what was to become one of the loves of his life: basketball.

Although at 5'8" or 5'9" John Q. wasn't particularly tall, he managed to outplay his counterparts. "I was a pretty good scorer for those days, usually high-point man. I went through all four years of high school with basketball. I played a little baseball, too, but I preferred basketball, because I could accomplish something in it.

"We had a coach (Clyde H. Payne) who was also superintendent of schools at that time. He was a big influence on my life because he took time to pay attention to my talent; he knew I came from a good home. He was just a great leader. He would talk to me about making good grades and things like that—which was not a problem for me—I got a lot of encouragement from him. There were a few people along the line that watched me, and they knew I had more than just the average possibilities because I always wanted to succeed. I wanted to get ahead. That was something that was embedded in my mind."

The Depression lasted through John's time in high school, but even in financial crisis, there were good times, as well. Like the time John and his friends put a farmer's mule in the cistern (he doesn't recall how they ever got the mule out), or somehow got a buggy on top of the roof of an old funeral parlor. According to one of his old teachers, John was always getting in trouble. Today when he talks about his exploits, his smile is understated, but there's a definite twinkle in his eye. His devilish sense of humor remains very much intact.

LIKE SO MANY DEPRESSION-ERA CHILDREN, JOHN WAS DEVELOPING AN UNSHAKABLE BELIEF IN THE NEED FOR HARD WORK.

Even in high school, John was goal oriented and determined, approaching everything he did with high intentions and dedication. His first real job was when he was hired by a farmer to plow. After a long day in the fields, John Q. headed for the barn at five o'clock. The farmer chastised him: "We work until sundown." Having been anxious to do a good job, John was embarrassed and humiliated to feel he had let his first boss down.

Like so many Depression-era children, John was developing an unshakable belief in the need for hard work. As attorney Bill Hart says, "He has the most incredible drive and determination to act on his vision."

After he graduated from high school in 1937 (in a class of 12 students), John's parents told him that they couldn't afford to send him to college, but that they would do everything they could to support his going. "They told me I should go, so I went and got a job, and I worked every summer in the wheat fields and things like that to get money."

John attended Monett Junior College and Southwest Missouri State Teacher's College (now University), where he received his teaching certificate in 1939. He taught science, history and physical education to junior high students at Cassville. "The first year I made $40 a month, and the second year I made $45."

Like his mentor, he coached basketball. "I took a little junior high team, and they had never played a basketball game in their life as a group. I taught 'em passes. Put 'em in nice clean uniforms. Got a schedule. We lost one game the first year and then went undefeated the second year." Winning was always in his cards.

John taught for just two years, but he continued to learn throughout his life, studying biographies to learn why great men did the things they did–what their strategies were, their strengths, their weaknesses. He has always believed you could learn by watching and listening. "There's an education on every corner if you look for it," he says.

As a young adult, John even served as a Cub Scout Cubmaster.

Eventually, he would leave behind the academic life, but he would still spend his days teaching and coaching, sharing his knowledge of the hotel business and what it takes to be a success.

The War Intervenes

On December 7, 1941, the bombing of Pearl Harbor by the Japanese sealed the United States involvement in World War II. And it also sealed John Q.'s fate, for in the war, John began to learn the rudiments of what would become his career.

In 1942, John signed on with Lytle-Green Construction of Des Moines, Iowa, to work as a cost accountant for the Alaskan-Canadian Highway, soon known as the Alcan Highway. Stretching 1,522 miles, from Dawson Creek, British Columbia, to Fairbanks, Alaska, the road was to serve as an inland route to Alaska. It was also called the Road to Tokyo.

The Alcan was John's first taste of the construction business. If he thought the Missouri winters were hard when he was a boy, they were nothing compared to Alaska. During the building of the highway, Alaska hit a record 72 degrees below zero. "It was pretty rough," he says.

The job was to take approximately eight months, with more than 10,000 military men and some independent contractors completing the job. The rugged conditions, combined with the distress of war, made it an uncommon challenge. But never one to turn down an opportunity, John made the best of the situation. During his time there, he invested in the stock market and saved every penny he earned. "By the time I came back from Alaska, between saving my paychecks and what I made on the market, I must have saved up about $60,000." A pretty impressive sum for that day or this, considering John was merely 23 years old.

When the highway was completed in 1943, the war was in full swing and John, in the Merchant Marines, served on a supply ship supporting the troops in both the Atlantic and the Pacific, achieving the rank of Lieutenant J.G. (junior grade).

John Q. is stingy with conversation about the war years, passing over it in just a sentence or two. And, when you think about it, why wouldn't he? That was some 60 years ago, truly a lifetime for many people, but not for John Q. Rather than be stuck in the past, as some might be, he'd rather talk about his life since then, the time when his life really began. The time when he started to become a developer.

A Great Idea and a Hard Lesson

When John came back to the States, he spent time in California trying to decide what he wanted to do. There he met a patent attorney with what John felt was a tremendous new idea: a mortarless brick that you could put together without spackle.

With John's background in construction, he saw it as a golden opportunity. He and the attorney took the idea back to Springfield, and got to work making it a reality.

He so believed in his product that he bragged to a competitor that he was about to put him out of business. His bravado came back to haunt him.

"TO ENTER BUSINESS YOU'VE GOT TO KNOW HOW TO WORK, AND YOU'VE GOT TO HAVE THE TRAINING AND THE EDUCATION."

"To enter business you've got to know how to work, and you've got to have the training and the education. But I was absent of experience and did not have enough capital. " John is honest about what his shortcomings were. In 1948, after just two years, the company went bust, his partner left town and John was saddled with the debt. He was 29 years old. "I lost my $60,000."

When you look at his success today, it's easy to underestimate such early difficulties. But consider that in the 1940s, a house might sell for $3,000; $60,000 was a princely sum and a huge amount to lose. It might have been enough to traumatize some people, perhaps enough to make them quit. But the loss didn't stop John. It was barely a speed bump in his path.

"I got down on my hands and knees to about six or seven big creditors and told them 'Look, I will pay this back, but you've got to give me three years.' When I said that, I had no idea how I was going to do it, but I said I'd do it. The alternative was that I would have to declare bankruptcy, and they wouldn't get their money."

The creditors agreed to his proposal to pay off the debt, and John spent the next two years rebuilding his life and paid off the debt a year early. "I didn't have a failure, but I didn't succeed," he says. Adversity just made him stronger.

The First-Class Lady

The last half of the 1940s were a tough time for John Q. business-wise. But the many troubles he had were outweighed by the personal decision he made to marry Juanita K. Baxter.

Juanita was raised on a farm in Marionville, Missouri, and came to Springfield to attend Southwest Missouri State Teacher's College (now University). Like John, she received a teaching degree. Although she began her teaching career in Marionville, she returned to Springfield to teach second grade at McDaniel School.

"She's a very stunning and gracious lady, who never met a stranger." Ask anyone who has ever met Juanita Kathleen Hammons, and you'll likely hear a similar description of the woman who is John Q.'s partner in life. Everyone agrees that Juanita K. is the epitome of a woman of style and substance.

"She has always been a first-class lady, and I say that out of re-spect," says John Q. He speaks of her with only the greatest admiration and consideration. Friends describe her as a charming hostess and tireless champion of the arts. She's a lovely, dark-haired woman whose stunning looks made a statement each time she entered a room.

"We met at a little dance at one of the hotels here, the Kentwood Arms," says John Q. They dated for a couple of years and were married September 2, 1949, at Westminster Presbyterian Church in Springfield.

She became his wife at one of the lowest points of John's business life. "She wanted to get married, but I didn't. Well, I guess I did. She said it was time to make a decision. Of course we were old enough to have some sense. We were 30. That's old enough to have some sense. I didn't have anything, but I told her that I was going to be successful in business, and business was going to be part of everything I do." It was clear that Juanita K. was willing to accept John's determination to succeed and to support him in every way. In his heyday of whirlwind traveling, when she didn't travel with him, she used to drop him off and pick him up at the airport from all his trips. And even after several decades of marriage, John told someone she still ironed his shirts.

Indeed, after 52 years, their friends describe her as the perfect partner, who has always been there for John and supported his constant quest for success.

Since she became "Mrs. Hammons" on September 2, 1949, Mr. Hammons has referred to her by that name. For about 10 years after their marriage, Juanita continued to teach second grade, but she eventually gave that up and focused on creating a life for herself that included a wide circle of friends and interests.

After Hours Happy Hours

While their early years included a good deal of socializing, John and Juanita participated in parties for different reasons. She enjoyed the dancing and chance to see friends. He was always table-hopping and working the room. "Mr. Hammons can move from the business dimension to being a very gracious, wonderful host at a party," says Marty McGahan, project manager of John Q. Hammons Hotels. "In the old days, he'd get together with the guys and play poker and let his hair down." There are tales of John Q. and his buddies, including car dealer Jude Montgomery, hanging out, playing Monopoly and eating Grape Nuts. They didn't have any money, so that was their splurge on Saturday night.

At one point, Mrs. Hammons complained that she and John always seemed to socialize with people who were 20 or 30 years older than they. She wanted to cultivate a younger group of friends.

"You know why I don't care to be with them? Because their priorities center around parties and socializing...Besides, I can something from people who are older."

Working His Way Back

With a new wife, no money and a boatload of debt, John was on the lookout for a way to regain his footing. By this time, he had devised the strategy that he would use for the long haul: Buy land, reserve the front part of the lot for commercial development and build residential lots on the rest.

John says he had the whole deal figured out, but he knew he would need help getting back on his feet. His first venture was to develop rental housing as a part of the FHA-insured Section 608 program. With veterans returning from the war and having babies, there was a need for multifamily housing, and John satisfied that need by building Village Gardens No. 1 in 1949 which was owned by Dan Savage, Sr., and Herschel E. Bennett. John didn't make much money on it, but he was staying afloat.

In 1950, he was ready to take on the second phase, Village Gardens No. 2. He figured he would need about $200,000. He sought the backing of sawmill and timber man J.V. Cloud.

Cloud asked John how much money they would make on it. "I told him I think we can make $100,000 to $200,000 building it. We'll own it, and it'll rent because there's a shortage of housing. I think we'll be able to sell it for a profit, of say, $250,000, in the next three years. Well, that was awful big for a young guy like me to tell him all that, but I believed it, because I could see it.

"J.V. would want to go over the costs, and I didn't have anything on paper, but I remembered every number. He'd ask how much for the steel, and I'd tell him. How much for the masonry, and I'd tell him. After our partnership was completed, I asked him why he backed me. He said, 'Because every time I would go up and down the sheet, I would ask you a number and the number was always the same.' I guess he figured I must know what I was doing."

Cloud gave him $1,000 a month to live on, and John ran the job. "He owned me lock, stock and barrel. But we built it, and it made $200,000. I got half, and he got half. And later we sold it, and we got another $200,000. And that's a true story."

All the while, John was investing in land. He built shopping centers, and residential developments and made a name for himself in Springfield. Not surprising, considering what a confident, outspoken young man he was.

The future looked brighter, for sure, but his success wasn't a sure bet—not for anyone, that is, but John. Many thought he was a wild thinker; in fact, there was always a method in his madness, but few people could see it.

In 1951, John was the featured Citizen of the Week in the Bias section of the *Springfield News Leader.* Here's the opening paragraph of the story:

"Thirty-two-year-old, cigar-smoking, hard-driving J. Q. Hammons is staking everything he has on the future of Springfield. He believes that Springfield has been undergoing a quiet and quite remarkable boom for the past five years, and that it will continue in this pleasant state for at least ten more years. If he has guessed right he will be well established at a still comparatively youthful age, but if the continued boom he foresees should fizzle, J. Q. will find himself with a number of mortgages and a stack of deeds-of-trust to acres of vacant real estate."

John was on his way, all right. One of his most memorable investments was Southern Hills, which he describes as the first "major master-planned residential district in southeast Springfield." He and partner Lee McLean bought seven farms of 1,000 acres and ultimately built the Southern Hills Shopping Center, as well as an upscale residential area where John Q. maintains his home today.

In all, he developed seven subdivisions, three shopping centers and three office buildings, including the John Q. Hammons Building. And then he hit a brick wall.

The Lava Theory: A Formula for Success

In a cover story of its June 2000 issue, *417 Magazine* says, "His penchant for buying land was rooted in the bedrock rule: They're not making any more land, so if you hang onto it long enough, you're bound to make a profit, either by selling it or developing it."

John Q. started practicing his theory early on. In 1957, at the tender age of 38, John Q. had already bought five farms that would become Highland Springs Country Club. He owned the land around the airport and a huge chunk of property in southeast Springfield. He was armed with land and ready to develop.

When he had returned from the war, Springfield was a small city: population under 50,000. But he could see its possibilities for growth, and he planned to take advantage of them. He based his development strategy on the way lava flows down a mountain. "Lava seeks its level, and so does a city's growth."

He took into account all the factors that he believed would affect the direction of growth, such as the waterways. He saw it would be cost prohibitive to deal with water drainage problems to the west. "I knew it would take 16 barrels of money to fix that, and I didn't want to touch that," he says. Besides, he could see clearly what path the citizens of Springfield were taking.

"Back in the '50s, all the freight trains would come right through the heart of town, but the town had grown so that soon people were moving into the outskirts. The money people were in the southeast part of the city, so that's where I wanted to go.

"Here came old Highway 60, and it meandered around down
south. I knew, even then, that this was the direction the city was
going. I used to take helicopters and go up and study cities, and
I'd spend two hours in the air sometimes. And I knew that this
was the way to go. I also knew that trains were a thing of the
past, and that we would need a freeway. But Springfield could
never raise the money to build such a road. We had to wait on the
state to do everything. I knew all that, but I could see what was
coming in the future."

Apparently, he was the only one who could see over the hill.

With 80 acres on Battlefield Road (that he bought for $1,000 an
acre), John proposed to the city to widen it all the way to
Glenstone Street in anticipation of what was coming. His ultimate
goal was to build a shopping center there. He had several key
stores lined up as tenants, and was anxious to get the road mapping to accommodate the new center.

"The head of the planning commission, Hank Denoble, did not see

---

**"HE HAS THAT GOD-GIVEN, INNATE ABILITY OF THE
OLD TEXAS OIL-CATTERS TO WALK ON A PIECE OF
LAND AND KNOW THERE WAS OIL UNDER THERE."**

---

the vision that I had. He thought that I was too progressive
trying to extend the city streets that far. I said, 'You're wrong.'" At
Denoble's urging, the planning commission voted against John.

He took it hard. When the city administration voted down his
proposal, he says, "That was the best defeat they ever gave me,
because it made me millions of dollars. I've never been a quitter.
It's a challenge to me. If they say it can't be done, well, then, I'll

do it." So he did.

No matter how many years it might take him, John Q. was like
lava. Once he started in a direction, there was really no stopping
him. Like every good survivor, he would ultimately outwit,
outplay and outlast any political mountain that got in his way. If
you want to see for yourself, just drop by Springfield and take a
look at the Battlefield Mall, located at 2825 South Glenstone, at
the corner of Battlefield Road.

"He has that God-given, innate ability of the old Texas oil-catters to
walk out on a piece of land and know that there was oil under
there," says project manager Marty McGahan.

Del Webb Goes Motoring

When John Q was just six years old, a concept was born that
would eventually change his life. In 1925, Congress created
legislation to develop a highway that would snake its way through
small towns in the Midwest and Southwest, ultimately connecting
Chicago to Los Angeles. Called Route 66, the highway has become
legendary, the source of a television series, inspiration for song
lyrics—"Get Your Kicks on Route 66"—and a vehicle for the
development of a whole new way of life on the road.

As the road developed, so did the businesses along Route 66. After
World War II, an increasing number of travelers led to the creation
of restaurants, service stations, and, most notably for John Q.,
lodging.

And John Q. wasn't the only one with success in mind. Another
man with sports in his heart and the wind at his back was developer Del Webb. Before John Q. set his first rabbit trap, Del Webb
was growing up in Fresno, California, preparing to become a
builder as well.

Webb started a construction company in Phoenix, Arizona, in 1928, and made a name for himself during the war building entire cities under defense contracts. His government work paid off, and he expanded into developing motels (a shortened version of the phrase "motor hotels") along Route 66. Traffic on the highway grew as American families took to the roads following the war and needed places to stay. In the beginning, lodging in small towns had been limited to tiny, isolated cottages that were all independent of each other and rented from a small office on-site. As traffic ballooned, the cottages gave way to motels that were built to house all guest rooms and facilities under one roof. Today, the remnants of these early themed accommodations are truly icons and are memorialized in books such as *The American Motel,* by Michael Karl Witzel.

Webb's Highway Houses, early travelers' havens, would shortly be the source of other inspiration: the seeds of John Q. Hammons' vision of the future. (And like John Q., Del Webb was a diehard baseball fan who would eventually become part owner of the New York Yankees in their most glorious winning days.)

Although Webb would ultimately get out of the Highway House business and into gaming, retirement communities and baseball, John Q. Hammons would soon take up where Webb left off.

John Q. Words of Wisdom

*Circulated at the request of John Q. Hammons

"You can achieve financial independence if you are willing to work hard, to learn, have the discipline to save, courage to invest and time to build."

Author Unknown

John Q. Hammons

The Early Days

Brother and sister James Quentin (February 24, 1919) and Wrenna Quentilla (December 20, 1921) grew up in The Depression in Fairview, Missouri.

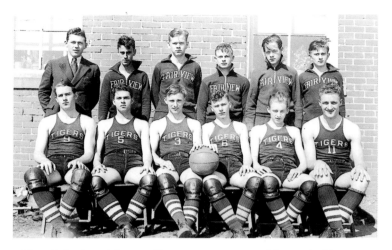

The Fairview Tigers (front row, second from left)

Quentin (left) was a top
scoring basketball
player in high school.

Monett Junior College (bottom right)

"Coach" Hammons took his
team to the top (1942).

A stint on the Alcan Highway taught John about construction.

...and at about -72 degrees, what cold really meant.

John Q. and Juanita K. (Baxter) Hammons.
September 2, 1949, Westminster Presbyterian Church,
Springfield, Missouri.

3

A Holiday Inn Success Story

A banker once turned John Q. down for a loan. Not to say that
John Q. believes in revenge, but years later, when he was amassing
his fortune, John Q. began to send the banker statements showing
how much money he was making. "Sometimes we made a mistake
in mailings," he says.

While John Q. Hammons was becoming a millionaire building
shopping centers and subdivisions in the Midwest, and Del Webb
was in the Southwest developing roadside hotels, Kemmons
Wilson was down south in Memphis, Tennessee, creating a brand
that would rival in awareness the names of Coca-Cola and Mickey
Mouse. Like John Q., Kemmons had humble beginnings, starting
out in business with a popcorn machine used in movie theaters.
As a homebuilder, Kemmons had moderate success in the late
'40s. In 1952, he loaded up the family station wagon and drove
his wife, Dorothy, and their five kids on a vacation trip to Washing-
ton, D. C. The trip was disastrous because they couldn't find
decent accommodations anywhere, but it was a piece of lucky
misery for Kemmons. The brief discomfort of that trip created a
lifetime of success for Wilson. A real entrepreneur's entrepreneur,
he saw a need and filled it, dreaming up the idea for a chain of
identical motels, comfortable accommodations you could count
on across the country, with the unique selling feature that kids
would stay free.

Kemmons went back to Memphis and had a designer come up with a concept. The designer had just seen the 1942 Bing Crosby movie, *Holiday Inn,* a story of a man who leaves big city life to create a beautiful country inn. The designer put the name *Holiday Inn* on his concept, and over the next two decades the name came to represent an international empire. The roadside chain of Holiday Inn hotels were travelers' favorites from their inception because they delivered a consistent product from coast to coast, at an affordable price, which at that time was about $4 to $6 a night. The hotels featured standardized accommodations and the promise of a clean room, free ice, in-room television and a swimming pool. Kemmons' original vision was to build 400 hotels across the country. It seemed like a big dream in the '50s, but when he left the company in 1979, there were approximately 1,750 hotels in more than 50 countries, and the company enjoyed $1 billion in revenues.

Meanwhile, events were taking place that would dramatically affect the rest of Kemmons' and John's lives, and link them inexorably in success. Simultaneous with Kemmons' founding of Holiday Inn, the Federal-Aid Highway Act of 1952 gave the interstate highway system its start. The act authorized $25 million in matching funds on a 50/50 basis with states. It was a small step, and not one that would change the face of America; however, when Dwight D. Eisenhower became President, he knew the importance of a nationwide road system, and he worked to develop a plan to provide funding for such an undertaking. It took four years to work out the details, but finally he signed the Federal-Aid Highway Act of 1956, a 13-year plan that would cost more than $25 billion and would be funded 90 percent by the federal government.

John Q. Goes West

While the President struggled with political foes of the interstate system, John Q. was on the road himself. Despite the obstacles John Q. had faced, by the end of the '50s, he was a millionaire, and was about to embark on the career that would make him not only wealthy, but also a legend.

Fed up with losing the war in Springfield over Battlefield Road, he took a trip out west and discovered Del Webb's Highway Houses. "They followed Route 66 all the way to New Mexico, past Amarillo and Oklahoma City and Tulsa. This was in about 1957, and I liked these Highway Houses, and I began to study that." By then, Del Webb had put Las Vegas on the map, with his construction of the Flamingo Hotel with mobster Bugsy Siegel. The Flamingo was the third hotel on what would become the flashy Las Vegas strip. He abandoned the Highway House development, leaving the field wide open for some up-and-coming developers.

The Last Puzzle Piece Falls into Place

Roy E. Winegardner, a plumber—or mechanical contractor, as he was known—from Springfield was learning about hotels the hard way. Roy, whose logo was a dripping faucet, had been the contractor on a hotel project in Huntsville, Alabama, and the project was about to go broke. In order to get paid, Roy had to buy it out, finish the hotel and run it himself. He opened the hotel as a Towne House. Unfortunately for Roy, just down the road was a Holiday Inn. He watched it outperform his Towne House, and, although the Holiday Inn certainly didn't represent anything in Roy's best interest there in Huntsville, he sort of liked what he saw. He opened his first Holiday Inn in Lexington, Kentucky.

"When I first met Roy Winegardner, he was wearing a pair of black chinos and a red Ban-Lon shirt, supervising a plumbing project," says Frank James, who retired from John Q. Hammons in 1990, as regional vice president. Roy was a slim, dark-haired man known for not mincing words. He knew construction, and had a habit of getting to the bottom line quickly.

Winegardner had been working with John Q. doing all the mechanical contracting on his homebuilding and shopping center
efforts. They ran into each other at the funeral of a friend. "Roy
heard I'd been defeated on the Battlefield deal. He told me about
this little hotel he'd built down in Lexington, and he said he was
thinking of getting into the hotel business in a big way. I said,
'Well, I am, too.'" John Q. was certainly interested in the possibilities of the motel business, having studied Del Webb's undertaking.
"I knew what was about to happen with the Interstate system,
and it looked like an opportunity."

Roy and John Q. took a trip to Memphis, where Kemmons and
Elvis were becoming the best-known names in town.

It was 1958, and Holiday Inn was growing fast. Wilson had developed a franchising plan for the hotels that included payment of a
one-time franchise fee, and then a royalty fee which amounted to
a percentage of each "room night" the hotel sold. It was a formula
that is intact today.

At the time that John Q. and Roy first visited Kemmons, they were
each successful in their respective businesses of homebuilding
and plumbing, and had each already developed a hotel or two.
Kemmons admired their tenacity and their accomplishments.
Nevertheless, Kemmons likes to embellish the story of their
meeting, claiming he pulled the wool over the eyes of two men
who would become major investors in his success. He laughs: "I
said, 'Well look here. We've got a teacher and a plumber, and they
want to buy some hotel licenses,'" says Kemmons. "I told Jack
Ladd and Jeff Mann (his franchise developers) to double the price
from $5,000 to $10,000. And these two guys bought ten franchises." Of course, the story has taken on a life of its own, but
Kemmons and John Q. both enjoy the folklore.

Thus far, Holiday Inn had sold 75 franchises. Kemmons gave John Q. and Roy 90 days to find 10 locations for their hotels. They first chose Cincinnati, Ohio. Roy and John Q., were in the hotel business for good. That year, they formed Winegardner & Hammons, and by the late '60s the company had developed more than three dozen hotels. Over the course of their partnership, Winegardner & Hammons would develop 67 Holiday Inn hotels, or what amounted to about 10 percent of the Holiday Inn system.

Those who know them might say the two were an unlikely partnership of opposites. But it certainly worked. John Q. found the sites and the money, and Roy handled the construction and operations. "You know why Roy and I stayed together? He was smart enough to know that what I did was valuable, and I was smart enough to know that what he did was valuable. So together, we were able to do so much. He knew a lot about construction, and I depended on that. I looked for the sites, got the money. I did all that. He didn't have the patience that I had. You deal with a banker, he doesn't know if he's going to make the loan or not. He's got to think about it. And he's not in any hurry, because he's paid to be cautious and careful. It takes somebody patient to deal with them. That was me."

"Roy was smart and I trusted his judgment. He was honest. He played the game straight, no question about that. We were honest. Period. You don't grow a company otherwise. You don't succeed otherwise. You don't succeed unless your integrity is above reproach."

Between Roy, the builder, and John Q., the developer, it was a match made for success. "Some of those early Winegardner & Hammons hotels had to be screaming homeruns," says regional vice president Joe Morrissey. "It was just like they printed money." In fact, Winegardner and Hammons were just two of the many people who became millionaires as a result of Holiday Inn hotels' popularity. Many people who started out working for Kemmons eventually became franchise owners. Everyone, it seems, wanted to get on the bandwagon.

And John Q. and Roy were building a bandwagon fast and furious; so fast, in fact, that they sometimes got the cart before the horse.

David Sullivan, a 40-year veteran of the industry and current member of John Q.'s board of directors, used to be in charge of franchise administration for Holiday Inns. He remembers that John Q. never quite followed the rules. "We had a long process where a potential owner would make an application, and then we'd study it, and take it to a committee for approval, and make sure the person who was building it was the right person, and we believed in the study and in the product he was going to do. It was a long, tedious process.

"Well, we'd get these applications in the mail from John Q. and we'd start the process, and when we'd call John he'd say, 'Don't worry about it; the hotel's already been built. In fact, it's opening next week.'"

Two Sports from Springfield, Mo

Perhaps one reason John doesn't like to follow the process is that he knows others are sometimes shortsighted about what will work and what won't. Like near Table Rock Lake in Missouri. Back in the late '50s, Hammons bought 1,500 acres located on Highway 13 beside the lake. He named it Kimberling City. At one point in the early Winegardner and Hammons history, John and Roy decided to build a hotel there. Roy's father liked to fish, and Roy didn't mind taking a turn with a fishing pole either. And, for some reason, John Q. has also always had an affinity for Table Rock Lake, even though he seldom takes time to do anything as relaxing as fishing.

The folks at Holiday Inn weren't keen on the project. John and Roy built a 60-room Holiday Inn anyway, which they operated for five years, through an impromptu company they formed called simply, Two Sports from Springfield, MO, Inc. They operated it for five years.

When it came to following their Holiday Inn franchisor's rules, not everyone could get away with such disregard for legalities. No doubt John Q.'s faster-than-a-speeding-bullet tactics have made more than one lawyer nervous. He still sometimes bypasses the application process. But John Q. can do what others cannot. He is so trusted to deliver a high-quality product, he's granted license in a world where few people can operate on such trust.

Boom Times, Bad Times

In 1969, business was booming. John Q. was turning 50, and he ran his empire on the phone and on the road. His airplane tickets were costing him about $30,000 a year, and his telephone charges weren't far behind. Indeed, in the early days, he traveled about 300 days a year, beating the bushes for deals and looking for land.

1969 was also the year John Q. founded John Q. Hammons Hotels. It was a fitting 50th birthday present to himself. While he and Roy had a successful partnership, they didn't always agree on locations or strategies. For example, John Q. had ideas about building in California; Roy wasn't interested in going that direction. He wasn't as convinced as John Q. of the potential out West.

They were still partners in Winegardner and Hammons, but the new arrangement allowed them to take some separate paths.

One path they did take together, though, was in 1970, when Winegardner and Hammons sold 23 hotels worth $50-60 million to Holiday Inns, Inc. The deal called for the hotels to be sold in exchange for Holiday Inn stock, a move that made John Q. and Roy among the largest stockholders of the hotel chain. Following the swap, John Q. was as eager as ever to develop hotels; Roy, who was more skeptical about the future of the development business, was less inclined.

Michael D. Rose, an attorney in Cincinnati, had worked with Winegardner & Hammons on the stock swap deal with Holiday Inns, Inc. Afterward, he became an integral part of their business. "In 1972, I left my law practice and actually went to work for Roy Winegardner. He and I formed a partnership, and it was sort of a side-by-side partnership with John Q. Hammons."

That year, Holiday Inn stock was selling for more than $56 a share. Life was good, especially for shareholders like Roy and John Q. It wouldn't last long.

In 1973, disaster struck. Until that time, Americans had little concern over the cost of energy. So called "gas guzzler" automobiles were a status symbol, and, because gasoline was cheap, it never crossed anyone's mind to worry about driving a big car that got eight miles to the gallon.

HE DIDN'T HAVE TIME FOR EVERYTHING TO BE OKAYED BY A ROOM FULL OF PEOPLE WITH WHAT HE CALLS "EXECUTIVITIS."

Then, in a startling turn of events in October, the members of the Organization of Arab Petroleum Exporting Countries (OPEC), placed an embargo on oil. Americans saw two things they never anticipated: gas prices over $1 per gallon and gas shortages. Suddenly, they were back to gas rationing, just like during the war. Lines of cars backed up for blocks waiting for service stations to open so that they would be first to get the limited supplies of gas.

For hotel companies, and, indeed, a company like Holiday Inn that depended on motorists driving to its hotels, the future looked questionable. The company's main business still involved the development of hotels, but in Kemmons' desire to be self-sufficient and to diversify, he had added an assortment of businesses that in some way, shape or form were related to the hotel company. There was a meat packing company to supply the hotels' restaurants, a drapery manufacturer to make drapes and bedspreads and a woodcraft facility to build furniture. There were steamships and buslines, and the list went on.

The stock price fell to just above $4 a share. Stockholders, including Roy Winegardner and John Q. Hammons, stood to lose their shirts if something didn't change. The decision was made to bring in new management, led by Winegardner. He took the role of vice chairman of Holiday Inns, Inc., and moved to Memphis to transform the company.

But what about John Q.? Well, no way was he getting involved in that corporate life. He was a man with a mission, and sitting behind a desk, going to meetings and following rules were not on his list. True entrepreneurs can't be bound by corporate nonsense. He didn't have time to have everything okayed by a room full of people with what he calls "executivitis."

John Q. Hammons had already served his time as president of the International Association of Holiday Inns (IAHI), an advisory board of franchise owners. Earle Jones, Mississippi Management Incorporated, was an early franchise owner who also sat in a number of meetings with John. "He was quite the sage, very much a forward-thinker in terms of macro-economic issues. He also was excellent at forming strategic scenarios about future Holiday Inn management moves and who was likely to be in what position."

"I had sat with the best people in the hotel industry, and I had learned from them what worked and what didn't," says John Q.

He wasn't about to give up the chance to put all that knowledge to work. He was in this world to build hotels, and build them he would, despite the oil embargo, despite claims that the industry was overbuilt, despite anything.

"Corporate life was not for John," says Ray Schultz, former chairman of Promus Hotels. John Q. had to be able to get out and about, travel the country, look for sites, seek out the next big deal, and build another slew of hotels. If Holiday Inn was to be saved, it was going to have to be Roy who did it.

A Lean Staff Gets a Lot Done

By 1973, John Q. was somehow running about 35 hotels with only a couple of people working in his office. It wasn't exactly what you'd expect of a millionaire hotel developer. But, of course, where John Q. is concerned, nothing ever is.

At least John Q. did have a CPA to handle his new hotel development and two women who kept the checkbook in the safe. All of the hotels were doing their own things. Eventually, John's team added an accounting system and started investing the money from the hotels daily." I think the first year we made $2 million to $4 million on interest," says Jacquie Dowdy, now an officer of the company, who has been with Hammons since his early years.

Through the years, although John Q. mostly shows his straight-to-business approach, Jacquie has had a chance to see his soft side. "When I first went to work for him, there were a lot of ladies who were Mrs. Hammons' friends that were older than she was at the time. They always had just a little bit of money, and they didn't know how to invest it. So John Q. would take that money from them and would pay them twice as much interest as they would get at the bank. That was his way of helping them without them knowing it."

Although few people would describe John Q. as a softy, it seems everyone has a personal story of his humanity. Like the hotel team member who was sick and needed to be hospitalized. John Q. arranged to get her a doctor and pay for the hospital bill. And there's the long-term employee, a bellman who was dying of cancer, and John Q.—the man with no time to spare—went to the hospital and spent an afternoon at his bedside.

Given the great respect he felt for his own mother, it's not surprising that he showed tremendous appreciation for another mother, Kemmons Wilson's wife, Dorothy. In 1970, Dorothy was named Mother of the Year and was recognized by President Richard Nixon in a White House ceremony. From that point on, John Q. sent her flowers every Mother's Day with a note that said, "Mother

---

"HE'S A FORCE TO BE RECKONED WITH AT ANY AGE."

---

of the year every year." Kemmons, who adored his wife, appreciated the gesture for more reasons than one: "It saved me a lot of money in flowers," he jokes.

John Q. obviously respected Dorothy tremendously, and feels a great sense of pride in bringing joy to her life. "Dorothy said to me a few years ago, after she had received the flowers one time, 'You've never forgotten.' I told her I never will." Indeed, on the Mother's Day following Dorothy's death in 2001, John Q. sent flowers to each of her daughters and daughters-in-law. It was a gesture Kemmons and his family will never forget.

Lee McLean, one of his business partners, says, "We used to have some bulldozer operators he liked, and he would call them to wish them Merry Christmas. He did that for 25 or 30 years. There may be some he still calls to this day."

So, are the tough negotiator and the soft-hearted guy two sides to John Q. Hammons?

John Q. knows how important it is to understand what makes people tick. He observes and studies people to find out how they think and what makes them do the things they do. And he believes that it's important as a leader that he maintain a position of authority, and to keep his distance. To him, showing care may show weakness, and that's not consistent with his need to be in control. But occasionally, there's a tiny hint that he may not be all business all the time.

Kemmons, who has remained a lifelong friend, obviously believes that John Q. has both head and heart. "I'd say he's the finest person that ever lived."

Build 'Em If You Got 'Em

No matter where John Q. is, he's always considering development. Once, he and friend Lee McLean and their wives were in St. Louis for a weekend. At the time, Lee and John Q. were considering building a shopping center in Springfield, and they had heard about the colonial style being built in St. Louis. They went into a supermarket, looking at the ceiling and noting how it was constructed. Nearby was a tall display of cans, stacked high in a pyramid. The store manager was walking across the aisle, and, seeing the two men staring at the ceiling, he looked up to see what they were looking at. As he gazed up, walking all the time, he ran right into the display, scattering the cans everywhere. John Q. and Lee began to laugh uncontrollably, and the poor manager never did realize what they had been looking at.

Put a "construction" site anywhere in John Q.'s view—even in a grocery store—and he'll study it. There's no question that development is where Hammons' heart lies. No matter what economic obstacle stands in his way, he pushes it aside and keeps on building. During the oil embargo that put gas in short supply and sent prices skyrocketing, during the '80s recession, and even at times when people said the hotel industry was overbuilt.

When Holiday Inn was at its peak of development, Hammons was the best "marketing tool" the company could have had. "He sold a lot of people on the value of the Holiday Inn franchise," says Jeff Mann, one of the company development staff who became a franchise owner. No doubt in his constant travels, Hammons introduced the hotel chain to a host of people. And as charismatic as he is, his enthusiasm must have been contagious.

By 1987, Hammons had made a fortune outwitting and outplaying other hotel developers. It put him on the *Forbes* magazine list of the 400 richest people in the country. In 1986, he made the list as number 383; within a year, he jumped to 268, with his worth estimated at $300 million. He shared the listing with people like his friend, Wal-Mart founder Sam Walton, and with another Missourian, August Anheuser Busch.

Interestingly, an article in the Springfield newspaper showed Hammons' age in 1988 as 65, four years off his actual age. When general counsel Debbie Shantz went to work for John Q., it was his birthday. She went into his office to get some papers signed, and he took three calls while she was there. He asked each caller, "Do you know what day it is? It's my birthday." Apparently, each person asked how old he was. Debbie recalls, "On the first call, he said he was 72. On the second call, he said 74. And on the third call, he said 73. I thought, oh my gosh, I've already committed to working here. What have I gotten myself into?" As Debbie has since discovered after working for John Q. for years, there's no doubt he knows the real number.

You wonder if his age-defying tactics are just for fun, or if they're deliberately intended to throw people off, allowing him to maintain the ultimate credibility as a force to be reckoned with. Such tactics hardly seem necessary, for, in fact, he is a force to be reckoned with, at any age.

Meanwhile, Back in Springfield

John Q. made a lot of his fortune outside his hometown. But he was simultaneously helping put Springfield on the map. Some people say that after his early defeat with Battlefield Road, John Q. was determined to come back to town and show everybody they were wrong about his ideas. Perhaps in the beginning that might have been true, but the fact is, Springfield is the perfect model for the kind of town where he likes to build hotels: a medium-sized city with a university. John Q. saw tremendous growth opportunity for the city, and he was determined to be a part of making it happen.

And besides, John Q. says Springfield is home. That's where Mrs. Hammons was, the rock behind the man, always loyal to John Q. and content to remain in the background, allowing him to have the limelight.

When John Q. began his tornadic career jaunt, Mrs. Hammons would always take him to the airport and pick him up from the 300-ish days he traveled. Once, he returned from beating the bushes for deals, and Mrs. Hammons suggested that perhaps he should stay home more. "She ran around with some women, and they'd advised her she ought to rein me in," says John Q. "They said I worked too hard and that we didn't attend enough functions together. I came home, and she gave me the once over. I said, 'Wait a minute. Who's been talking to you?' She named this woman, and I said I knew where her husband was, that he was at the pickle works or the steel mill or something. So I said, if you want to join that crowd, it's fine with me, but I'm not going. We had a running joke between us that she let several lawyers die without getting a divorce!"

Mrs. Hammons sometimes traveled with John Q., but as years went on, she remained home enjoying her friends, taking care of her yard, enjoying basketball games and supporting the arts. She has been instrumental in planning more than one gala (most of which make the front page of the newspaper in Springfield).

Although vacations for John Q. are few and far between, on one occasion, he and Juanita did plan a trip to Hawaii. It was a get-away, supposedly, but John Q. began to plan an itinerary that would allow them to combine site-seeing with looking at land. "If we do it this way, we can save time and be able to look at some property," he told her. She replied, "Mr. Hammons, I've saved about all the time I'm going to save." She has a sense of humor as well.

Today, more than 50 years after they married, Mr. and Mrs. Hammons continue to show the greatest respect for each other. Friend and president of Drury University, Dr. John Moore says, "I've never seen a relationship that I thought was more perfect." They have grown up, and grown old together.

The Wells Go Dry

John Q. hasn't met many brick walls he couldn't tumble, but in the late '80s and early '90s, he confronted an obstacle he couldn't overcome. In a 1996 magazine article, he said he'd hit a wall that he couldn't penetrate: The banks had all closed.

"I TOLD ALL OUR MANAGERS THAT WE WERE GOING TO STAY IN THE QUALITY BUSINESS."

It was a tough time for a man who lives for one thing and one thing only: building. And the problem with the kinds of hotels John Q. builds is this: they're a pretty expensive proposition, ranging in the tens of millions.

Many hotel developers had begun building economy, or budget hotels, that eliminated huge commercial space, restaurants and other features that would drive up construction and operating costs. These "budgets" were not on the drawing board at John Q. Hammons' offices. He saw them as cannibalizing his own upscale hotels, and he didn't see them as a good long-term investment.

"I was at our Manager's conference in Fresno, California, in the early '80s, and I told all of our managers that we were going to stay in the quality business. I said I've made up my mind that the day is coming that there will be so many budgets built that you won't believe it. The price of entry is low, and you don't have to be very smart to do 50 or 100 rooms. We're not going to travel there. We're going to get with the colleges, universities and state capitals. We're going to get into solid markets, and we're going to build quality hotels."

As much as he considered them a better investment, he also simply enjoyed building showcases, hotels that had pizzazz. Economy hotels you could build for $5 million. John Q.'s were in the range of $35 million. And there certainly were no water features (John Q.'s favorite hotel design element) in budget hotels.

Besides his commitment to upscale hotels, John Q. has been wedded to the concept of convention centers that he believes drive business for the city as well as his hotels. One of his latest projects is a $55-million Renaissance Convention Hotel in Tulsa, Oklahoma. Scheduled to open in early 2003, this is his fourth Renaissance hotel. His other three are in Richardson, Texas (adjacent to the Eisemann Performing Arts Center), in Oklahoma City (connected to the Myriad Convention Center) and in Charlotte, North Carolina. After the Richardson opening, Hammons received a note from Bill Marriott, Jr., that said, "Superb. Keep up the good work!" The Oklahoma project was one that required a

helicopter reconnaissance flight, one of John's favorite ways to
get a view of how the city was developing. John Q. also had
"inside information" about how the city would grow: His friend
Sam Walton, told him 20 years before that "by the year 2020 the
center of Tulsa's retail activity would be 10 miles southeast of 71st
Street and US 169." Near his hotel.

But those are recent successes. Back to the '90s. Money was
scarce. And while it was true he had invested some of his own
money in hotels before, to do things on the scale he liked to do
them, Hammons had to find an alternative.

Going Public

In 1994 John Q. Hammons did the unthinkable. He put a portion

---

"I CAN GO BANKRUPT, OR I CAN GO PUBLIC."

---

of his fate in the hands of a board of directors. It wasn't something that he relished, but he needed money to build hotels. As he
bemoaned, "I can go bankrupt, or I can go public." He seemed to
have almost equal disdain for both options. But at this point, even
the John Q. Hammons name wasn't sufficient to garner the capital
he sought. He decided to go public.

Because he felt he was "just a farm boy" who might not curry
favor with the "Wall Street types," John Q. hired a former Holiday
Inn executive to be president of the company. Together, they
formulated a plan that qualified John Q. Hammons Hotels, Inc., for
a seat on the New York Stock Exchange. On November 23, 1994,
the initials JQH became a stock symbol for John Q. Hammons.

The good news was that it meant money in the till for more hotel
development. The company offered more than six million shares

for more than $100 million. The bad news was it also meant red tape. John Q. especially doesn't appreciate having to go to anyone for permission to build a hotel. After all, he feels, it's his company. And fortunately for John Q., he retains about 77 percent of the stock of the company. Unfortunately, he still has to have board approval, and on occasion the board does make calls with which he doesn't agree.

In 1998, for example, they called for a moratorium on development, a move that put a crimp in John Q.'s style. During the late '90s he had been doing deals right and left, and had developed 24 hotels since the company went public. When the board called a halt, it put John Q. in the position of protecting his good name.

In some cases, there were deals for which he had given a handshake, such as the convention center hotel in North Charleston,

---

NO MATTER WHAT THE ECONOMY DOES, NO MATTER WHAT THE CIRCUMSTANCES, JOHN Q. KEEPS ON FORGING AHEAD.

South Carolina. No moratorium would stop John Q. from fulfilling an obligation he had made. He took the personal position that he had made a commitment and that he would never renege on a deal. He certainly wouldn't put his name at risk. Considering that his reputation enables him to make deals no one else could make, certainly not on a handshake, he always lives up to what he's said he'll do...and more. "If you don't do what you say, word of that will travel all around the country. I've never had that kind of reputation, and I never will." His strategy was to live up to those commitments by using his own capital. The public company continues to manage his private hotels.

Going his own way was nothing new to Hammons. In the '70s, when Roy Winegardner had put the brakes on development for

Winegardner & Hammons, John Q. just developed under his other company. And when the board of his now-public company told him not to develop, he did the same thing. He simply began developing through his private company.

No matter what the economy does, no matter what the circumstances, John Q. keeps on forging ahead. He's weathered a lot of storms, and he never thinks a negative thought. Experience has taught him that he will prevail, no matter what fate throws at him.

In the long run, no one tells John Q. not to do something. It only fuels his desire. He takes up the challenge and becomes determined to prove he can do what others cannot. And for the most part, he can.

And so it goes. Call it determination or just downright stubbornness. It's a trait that has landed him squarely in the middle of the legends of the hotel industry. By 2000, John Q. had more than a lifetime of achievements. He won the first lifetime achievement award ever presented by Holiday Inn, as well as the first Connie award for achievement awarded by Hilton Hotels to anyone outside the company. The crowning moment of his success may at one time have been the award he and Roy Winegardner received from the University of California-Los Angeles Fifteenth Annual Hotel Industry Investment Conference. Or it may have been the party at The Chateau for his 40th anniversary in the business. Knowing John Q., more than likely, the highest achievement of his career is still in the offing.

John Q. Words of Wisdom

*Circulated at the request of John Q. Hammons

The Bridge Builder

An old man going a lone highway,
Came at the evening, cold and gray,
To a chasm, vast and deep and wide
Through which was flowing a sullen tide.
The old man crossed in the twilight dim,
The sullen stream had no fears for him,
But he turned when safe on the other side,
And built a bridge to span the tide.

"Old Man," said a fellow pilgrim near,
"You are wasting your time with building here,
You never again will pass this way,
Your journey will end with the closing day.
You have crossed the chasm, deep and wide,
Why build you this bridge at evening tide?"
"Good friend, in the way I've come," he said,
"There followed after me today
A youth whose feet must pass this way.
This stream that has been as naught to me,
To the fair-haired youth might a pitfall be.
He, too, must cross in the twilight dim,
Good friend, I am building a bridge for him."

Author Unknown

4

All in the Course of a Day's Work

His career has been like a ride on a 120-mile-per-hour roller coaster. Yet he's done it all with an amazingly simple system: a yellow legal pad. A red marker. Folders held together with rubber bands. A handful of quarters for phone calls. They don't sound like the tools a modern businessman would necessarily use to make his fortune, but they're all John Q. needs to keep $200 million in development going all the time.

John Q. likes the wide open spaces, like the one he sees from his top-floor office in the nine-story John Q. Hammons Building, his Springfield headquarters. His office is big; probably 40 by 25 feet, taking up a corner of the building and surrounded by windows.

At any given point, he shares his office with a dozen or so (seasonally appearing) docile wasps, which he ignores. He has no time to deal with petty annoyances. At one side of the room is his desk, unused except as a resting place for trophies and memorabilia. The book shelf, credenza and table are also covered with gifts and mementos: awards his hotels have won, lifetime achievement plaques, the book *Stormin' Back*, about Norm Stewart, a bronze Payne Stewart sculpture commemorating the golfer's induction into the Missouri Sports Hall of Fame. And there are balls, including a basketball signed by Walt Frazier, a Stan Musial baseball card and a pen holder recognizing coach Tom Landry. On top of the television, there is a Wheaties cereal box with John Q.'s picture on it, a remembrance of a hotel conference he attended. A small, framed newspaper article recounts the opening of the Fort Collins Holiday Inn in 1984. And a magazine, *Elite Home & Lifestyle,* gives some hint of where he gets ideas. Most appropriate, a pillow inscribed with the words: We've Had Our Ups and Downs.

You get the feeling that to John it's all extraneous. Not that he's not grateful for gifts or accolades. He simply doesn't devote energy to anything outside his development efforts. He probably doesn't keep the memorabilia for sentiment. And he certainly doesn't keep them as something to show off, either. The only thing he takes the time to show off is photos of his properties.

The real heart of the office is the gigantic conference table, 10 by six feet, loaded down with construction plans, about 50 of them, rolled and rubber-banded, and no telling how old.

John Q. sits at one end of the table, where he keeps his multiline phone, his fabled yellow legal pad, red marker, paper clips, a stack of business cards (also held together by rubber bands), and a glass of water that's placed there by his assistant each morning before he arrives. Just in front of him is a wooden hand with the thumb and little finger extended, holding what else—rubber bands—and proclaiming, "Hang Loose."

Dressed for Success

Any day you catch John he will be dressed for business, wearing one of his 300 ties—just about all gifts from friends, and all outrageously colorful. Even though it's February, he may be wearing the tie with Christmas lights on it, but no matter; he still looks every inch the gentleman, wearing his jacket in the office all day. Mark Snyder, head of Embassy Suites Hotels, says "In all his traveling, I have never once seen him look ruffled; never seen him with a hair out of place. Never."

Recently, he's traded dress shoes for a pair of black walking shoes, a small concession to his 83 years, and the fact that he still keeps a healthy pace. Remarkably, he still has all his thick, wavy hair. (It's more hair than most people enjoy for even a brief time in their lives!) It's all silver now, but still swept up in a style that adds several inches to his height. His trademark glasses haven't changed for decades, and he still likes to keep a good tan.

Besides the ties, he's not a flashy guy personally. His office isn't fancy or plush. His staff is small. In fact, none of what surrounds John Q. is what you'd expect of a wealthy entrepreneur. It is what you'd expect of a man who believes in hard work and is not much impressed with the trappings of royalty (which in Springfield, he pretty much is).

He's so down to earth, it's sometimes hard for people to believe that what they see is what they get. "We've gone through several audits with the IRS," says Jacquie Dowdy, who takes care of the accounting for his personal businesses. "The IRS is certain we must be hiding something, because they can't believe a man that makes that kind of money doesn't have yachts and condos and houses all over the place."

The Work Day

"It costs me a lot of money just to sleep," says John Q. So, after just six hours of sleep—from midnight to 6 a.m.—he's ready to roll. His assistant and his receptionist are there when he arrives at his office at 8 a.m., and they juggle his schedule and his calls. That's no mean feat considering that he makes and gets about 80 calls a day. The traffic in and out of his office is constant, and most meetings last generally no more than minutes. The whirlwind ends for most when he leaves at 4:50 p.m...to miss the rush-hour traffic, which, unquestionably, would waste his precious time. And don't think work stops just because he leaves the office. He's working six nights out of seven. Architect Steve Minton, some of Hammons' 56 hotel general managers and other business associates get calls up until 11 p.m. No one seems to mind. In fact, most everyone appreciates the personal calls and understands that when the business day is officially over, John Q. sometimes just needs someone to talk to.

Bill Killian, of Killian Construction, who builds some of John Q.'s projects is on the receiving end of those calls at times. When the Hammons' tornado leaves town, Killian often travels with him.

Bill, who is a young 47, describes one of their trips on the construction company's private plane: "We were planning to leave at 7 a.m. for the east coast to look at sites. I went to bed early, knowing I'd have to be up at 5 for our flight. At 11 o'clock that night, though, the phone woke me up. It was John, making sure we were on for the next day. We chatted for a while. Then I went back to sleep. We left at 6:45 a.m. for Peoria, Illinois, where a developer picked us up, and we toured the city and the site. Then we flew to Concord, North Carolina, and had a lunch meeting in a conference room at the airport with a mayor and city representatives. At about 2 o'clock, we flew to Charleston, South Carolina, where another mayor picked us up and we talked about a hotel deal. We looked at the site, then flew to Columbia, South Carolina, stayed in one of John Q.'s hotels, and were talking business until about 10 o'clock. By then, I was pretty dead, and John said he had to go to his room to make a phone call. The next morning he had a 7 a.m. meeting, and then we flew back to Springfield. I was tired! I'm 47, and he's 83, and I can barely keep up with him!

Ted Coleman, vice president, owner and franchise services, Marriott Hotels, echoes: "He's 82, I'm 42. I wish I had his energy, his passion for business and quality is second to none."

Never mistake what John Q. does for work. To him, this is fun, this is life. And as the old saying goes, "to be happy, get someone to pay you to do what you love to do." If that's true, John Q. must be one happy fella.

Where's John?

One time, Ray Schultz, former chairman of Promus Companies, was at a meeting with John Q. in Lake Tahoe. "We were right in the middle of our meeting, and John Q. got up and left. About an hour later, he called me in the meeting and said, 'Ray, can you do me a favor?' I said, 'John, where are you?' He said, 'Phoenix.' We didn't even know he was gone. He went on to say, 'Look, I left my airline tickets in my room there. Could you go get them for me?' I went to his room, and there was this huge stack of airline tickets

---

"JUST PUT ME ON A FLIGHT, ANY FLIGHT. I'VE GOT BUSINESS EVERYWHERE."

---

for flights all over the place, held together in a rubber band. You see, when John was at the airport, if a flight got delayed, he'd just walk up to a ticket counter and tell the agent, 'Just put me on a flight, any flight. I've got business everywhere.'"

Business everywhere, and business every minute. John Fulton, vice president of design and purchasing for John Q. Hammons hotels, tells a story about John Q. (during his early Springfield development years) having a meeting with Springfield electrical contractor Phil Roper.

Roper got a call from Hammons asking Phil to meet him at 5 a.m. the next morning at a 24-hour restaurant. When Phil arrived, John Q. was scribbling on a pad, and Phil didn't want to interrupt his train of thought, so he just waited. Every so often, John Q. would mumble, 'It's just terrible, terrible.' Finally, Phil asked, 'Just what's so terrible?' Hammons looked up and replied, 'I could just get so much more done if I didn't have to slow down to sleep.'"

Jim Anderson, president of the Springfield Area Chamber of Commerce, says, "If ever there was a poster child for hard work and determination, it's John Q. Hammons. I've never met anyone in my life that's more determined, more focused. When I say 'hard work,' to him it is his life."

A Down-to-Earth Visionary

If you travel with John Q., don't expect to see him demand the royal treatment. He's a down-to-earth person who flies coach and buys his clothes off the rack. He's been known to show up at a hotel in his walking shoes carrying a shopping bag. "I left my stuff in a locker at the airport," he'd say. For a quick trip in and out, why did he need to carry a suitcase?

He doesn't live ostentatiously, doesn't dress like a millionaire, and doesn't expect fanfare. His favorite treats are vanilla ice cream and V-8 cocktail juice. Most of the time he eats the same thing for lunch each day, something light like soup and cottage cheese. He's not even familiar with many of the things we consider daily conveniences.

Attorney Bill Hart once took a road trip with John Q., and they stopped at a Wendy's restaurant for lunch. "John looked around and said, 'What do they serve?' I said, 'I'm getting a chicken sand-wich.' So John said, 'Okay, that sounds fine to me.' Afterward, he said, 'This is pretty good. Do they have these everywhere?'"

Don't Sweat the Small Stuff

He's so busy traveling around he has little time to experience the everyday stuff most "regular" folks do.

One time, Mrs. Hammons called the office to ask John Q. to bring home a box of crackers. Jacquie was giving him a ride home, and he asked her if they could stop at the grocery. She asked if he would like her to go in for him. "I could tell he was relieved. He wouldn't have any idea where to get those crackers. He makes such big deals, he doesn't know where to begin in the real world. I've actually heard him ask a clerk, 'Are those razor blades one million or two?'"

Despite his unassuming style, Hammons is a larger than life figure, a man who has made his mark. Stephen P. Joyce, executive vice president, owner and franchise services, Marriott Hotels, says, "There are a couple of guys in the industry that, when it's all said and done, it's nice to be able to say, 'I knew him,' and John Q. is one of those guys."

Scott Tarwater, vice president of sales and marketing, John Q. Hammons Hotels, occasionally goes to a Southwest Missouri State University Lady Bears basketball game with John Q. "We'll go to a game on Saturday night, and if there are 7,000 people there, he knows half of them," says Tarwater. "The game starts at 7:15 p.m., but you have to get John there at 5:45 so he can make it around to all the people who want to say hello, or touch him and shake his hand. You have to go from the front door through the throng of people to the steps, and at every bleacher, every seat, you have to stop." As one person describes it, it's "like walking through the Vatican with the Pope."

If He Wants It to Be True, It's True

And some say that if John Q. wants something to be true, it's true. Like his birthday, which is legally February 24, but which he likes to celebrate on the 22nd. (Some people think it's because he wants to share a birthday with the Presidents.) Even the name John Q. is a piece of wishful thinking. But that's a later chapter.

He certainly has a way of making things happen his way. Of pushing the limits, and sometimes breaking the rules. He's a storyteller and a historian, a student of people and their motives. He's a visionary, a gambler, and, at heart, a guy who loves to wheel and deal. He doesn't have everyone's love, but he does have their respect. He's one of the few business people who can still get deals done on a handshake.

A Global View

Some, including John Q., say he's just a country boy, but there's no hay on his overalls. He's a history buff with a penchant for biographies. He reads about great people because he believes he can learn from them. His favorite light reading is *The Wall Street Journal,* or *Fortune* magazine. He stays on top of the economic situation. Politics seem to matter little to him: He just wants to know which one is the winning side.

> "HE'S LIKE A CURIOUS CHILD WHO WANTS TO INVESTIGATE EVERY NEW TOY. ONCE HE'S FIGURED OUT HOW IT WORKS, HE'S OFF TO THE NEXT NEW IDEA."

Hotels are his life, but that's not to say that John Q. hasn't been diverted in other and sometimes strange directions. In his 60 years in business, he's never been one to pass up anything that looked like a good opportunity. He's been right, and he's been wrong, but you can't say it hasn't been interesting.

He's like a curious child who wants to investigate every new toy. Once he's figured out how it works, he's off to the next new idea. That means he's not only been successful in development, he's also dabbled in other areas. Of course, every bit of it starts—and ends—with real estate.

A Bolo Tie and a Business Suit

In the early days of Holiday Inn, one of Kemmons Wilson's partners was Wallace Johnson. Johnson, a devout Baptist, helped guide the hotel company to inject religion into its business. Every hotel room featured a Gideon Bible, and the company even had a Chaplain-on-Call program to minister to guests. One of the things that the company was very restrictive about was anything associated with gambling, considered by some to be immoral. But that didn't stop John Q. He was headed for Nevada.

John Q. owned 20 acres of urban renewal property on 6th Street at Wells Avenue and I-80 in Reno. (That's how he describes everything, in streets and expressways.) "This was at the time Howard Hughes was remodeling the Sands in Vegas," says John.

Hammons was going to build a 14-story hotel with a casino next door. To do that, he would need a gaming license. The process required him first to go before the gaming board in Carson City. Having cleared that hurdle, an appearance before the gaming commission was next.

"My lawyer and I went in and I was wearing a suit and a bolo tie," says John Q. "Right in front of us were about 18 guys who arrived in three limos, wearing black suits. They took up the first three rows. They were there on behalf of Howard Hughes." Hammons says he got his license just after Hughes, and went on to build the hotel and the casino.

"We had to have a real small door to the casino, because Holiday Inn was so restrictive about gaming that they didn't want anyone to be able to see the casino from the hotel." After Wallace Johnson's retirement, Hammons widened the connecting door to 40 feet.

(Ironically, Holiday Inns, Inc., eventually bought Harrah's casino company and got smack dab into the gaming business in all the major markets.)

The casino still stands today, and that wasn't John Q.'s last gaming venture. When Illinois was going to issue 10 gaming licenses, John Q. was a prime candidate, and the people at Harrah's knew that. He approached Harrah's to be a partner.

"I had been talking with Caesar's Palace, but the deal didn't work out," he says. "So I flew down to Memphis and met with Phil Satre, the head of Harrah's, and we talked for about three hours. We had a deal on the spot." The intention was to build a casino/ hotel in Joliet, Illinois. "I got the friendly approval of the city because I had a Holiday Inn hotel there."

John's venture into gaming has been lucrative, but he almost seems to have a "been there, done that" attitude toward the business. He's dabbled, and now he sits back and collects his money while he's on to the next adventure.

The Food Groups

John Q. has dabbled in some diverse food groups. One of his food forays was Burger Station, a double drive-through hamburger restaurant. Everyone in Springfield had said Burger Station made the best hamburger around, and John Q. likes that kind of public endorsement. But after a while, the restaurants just didn't cut the mustard. It seems that with a hamburger stand, the hassles are just about as great as they are with a hotel in terms of hiring and all, but the bottom line is only $100,000 or so compared with a hotel that makes $4 million. Small potatoes for John Q.

This is not to say that Burger Station was a failure. Having the knack that he did, he turned it into a lease, so he owned the buildings and he got about $200,000 to $300,000 because he received a percentage of what they sold. Sounds a lot like the old Holiday Inn formula.

Sometimes a sideline is a means to an end, a way to support a mainstay hotel. For example, with land around the Springfield airport (Mrs. Young's apple orchard purchased in 1954), John Q. was in a prime spot to develop a hotel. In 2001, Hammons built the Springfield Courtyard by Marriott. Since the hotel is off the beaten track, Hammons put in a restaurant, the Cafe, next door.

More recently, John Q. has decided to invest in a franchise restaurant operation, Cheddar's, a casual dining chain that's privately owned and has about 40 properties across the country. He got there through a friend, his "Florida Connection," Bill Hickman, a native Missourian who relocated to Florida and has done some development there with John Q. Along with Hickman and two other partners, John has purchased franchise rights for west coast Florida, with a right-of-first-refusal for the rest of the state. By year end 2002 he will open his first Cheddar's restaurant in Brandon, outside Tampa.

Hickman told John about the restaurant chain, and invited him to get involved. John Q. undertook a research project, asking people on airplanes and other travel venues if they had ever eaten at Cheddar's. Says Hickman, "John was building a hotel in Tulsa, and they had a Cheddar's across the street. He watched the crowds outside, and that helped him decide it was a good venture."

All the World's a Stage

Try to get John Q. to tell you about his role in the 1939 play, "Running Wild," and he'll caution, "Now you're digging too deep." But perhaps his interest in theater explains his investment in the theater business. Or maybe it's because he watched the evolution of Branson, Missouri, into a tourist destination and decided he might like to replicate that town's experience in Myrtle Beach, South Carolina. As a result, he got into the "stage" business there with two ventures.

In the first instance, he purchased five franchises for IMAX theaters, which feature large screens and larger-than-life films. His first IMAX theater opened in Myrtle Beach in 1995, and he underwrote the production "Great American West."

At the same time the IMAX was opening its doors, John also opened the Palace Theater, the largest domed building in the state including the capitol. The 2,640-seat theater was to feature name entertainment. In fact, for five years straight, the Rockettes dancing troupe performed there.

Worms, Anyone?

When you're John Q. Hammons, you have a chance to review lots of opportunities, some good, some not so good. In the course of his career, John Q. has seen his share of out-of-the-ordinary plots to make money. A few stand out. Like the worm deal.

After John Q. made an unsuccessful bid to get Battlefield Road widened, he got an unusual offer for the use of his land. "Three

"THAT'S A TRUE STORY."

guys came in here one day with an offer to rent my 100 acres to farm worms that they could sell at Table Rock for fishing. I said, 'What are you going to pay me?' And they said, 'We can't pay much, but if we get successful, we'll pay you some.' I turned them down, but can you believe that? That's a true story."

Another unusual business he's encountered was a factory in Monett, Missouri, that transformed chicken manure into pellets of fertilizer. The venture didn't pan out for John Q., but for years Hammons kept a bag of fertilizer in his office.

More deals than not end up in file 13, either because he's not interested or because one of his team protects him from potential scams and people of questionable character. Sometimes he asks his team, "So, how are the thieves today?" He jokingly references people who would take advantage of him, but undoubtedly that 16-year-old bully who stole his rabbits is never far from his mind.

Back Home

Although he may stray into a variety of realms, John Q. always comes back to "dance with the one who brought him": he is first, last and always, a developer of hotels. He certainly takes every opportunity to jump on what looks like a bandwagon—or rather, to create a bandwagon—but the lure of the hotel business never loses its attraction. The chance to envision a structure, to imagine a panorama, to create a skyline and to add beauty to a city is something that he can't resist. So no matter what he dabbles in as a sideline is merely that, a short departure from his first and only true love: hotels.

John Q. Words of Wisdom

*Circulated at the request of John Q. Hammons

How to Make Money
GO TO WORK!

Author Unknown

**

There is no limit to how far you can go if you don't get hung up arguing about who should get all the credit for an idea.

Author Unknown

**

"United we can move mountains."

Author Unknown

5

No Guts, No Glory, or How to Develop Just About Anything

"I used to have an accountant who would offer a prayer before he'd cross the street," says John Q. Just a guess: That person may not have lasted long in the John Q. Hammons organization, where risk-taking is a vital part of the game. In his lifetime, he says he's borrowed somewhere in the neighborhood of $3 billion.

Nevertheless, he won't describe himself as a gambler; most of his risks are well calculated, and besides, they're executed in the hotel industry, a business that, after 40 years, he knows extremely well. The hotel industry can be a very lucrative business, as it was in the booming '60s and late '90s, and it can be very challenging, as it was during the gas crisis in the '70s, the 1991 Gulf War and the recession just prior to and after the 9-11 tragedy of 2001.

Through it all, John Q has followed his own unique formula for success. Having, as he says, "lived through five recessions," Hammons has had plenty of time to study the cyclic nature of things and to develop a philosophy that is unwavering. While he does believe in playing the market, he cautiously refers to it as "Vegas on Wall Street." He'd rather invest in something he knows will escalate in value: land. "I buy land early, and if the market goes that way, I build on it. If it doesn't go that way, I sell it, and inflation bails me out."

What's clear is that John Q. can be an amazingly patient man. Although he certainly is a driver, pushing to get things done in a hurry, he's proven that he can be incredibly patient when it comes to holding onto land for literally decades until the most advantageous time to build. In one case, he bought land in 1954 and didn't build a hotel there until 2000. Now that's patience.

Rule 1: Pick the Right Location

Typically, when he's considering where to develop, he focuses on what are considered to be secondary or tertiary markets, not a Chicago or Atlanta, but places like Little Rock, Arkansas; Tulsa, Oklahoma; and North Charleston, South Carolina. Those are areas where he believes he can build a hotel that will be the dominant property in the area, and will also serve as a true cornerstone of the community. His goal is to be a big fish in a middle-sized pond.

He picks state capitals, or cities where there are universities. "When your economy does this up and down, you have to guard against it. The economies of state capitals and universities stay the course because the politicians still prevail and kids still go to school. That's how come I was to develop that approach."

"Many, many times I go into these places, and I get the city interested in building a convention center with their money. They sell municipal bonds to foot the bill. Then I build a hotel adjacent. When I do that, then I don't have to raise all that money. It's a

---

"WHEN HE CHOSE A SPOT, IT WAS PRETTY SURE TO BE A SLAM DUNK."

---

good deal for the counties or the cities because it increases sales tax; the momentum of the business is income-producing for them.

So they have their motel tax and they have their sales tax. Plus, they have the welfare of the county, because we employ a lot of people. When we build a big hotel and convention center we're employing around 200 people all the time. That's the same as a little factory moving in and setting up business. So not only do you take care of the people that need to have meetings and places to stay and continued increasing commerce activity, but you also provide employment for a lot of locals. So, I do that when I can.

"That's the case in Charlotte. I'm looking over a golf course, and I'm right half way between the airport and the big mall and the race track in Charlotte. Three miles away is the University of North Carolina at Charlotte." Pointing in one direction he says, "Here's I-85, and Charlotte's Motor Speedway. When the state designs a beltline freeway around the city, that's what provides the vehicle for the people to come."

George Falls, restaurateur and one of the early Holiday Inn team members, says, "It was my job to pick locations, but John Q. knew more about picking them than I did. When he chose a spot, it was pretty sure to be a slam dunk."

John Q. finds real estate the same way he once trapped rabbits. He gets up early and goes looking. What he wants is to buy early, before anyone else realizes that a location is prime. That's been his habit throughout his career. One of his favorite ways to do business is to start with a big chunk of land that he thinks is a likely spot for a hotel. Then he holds onto the property until someone else wants it. When the price is right, he sells them a piece, retaining enough land to build his hotel on. He uses the profit he makes on the land to fund the construction of the hotel. He acts like it's a cinch.

Not everybody agrees with John Q.'s picks, but sooner or later they usually find out he was right.

He is famous for doing market research from a helicopter or airplane. Circling a city, he looks for active areas or obvious trends in development. From the air, he can see where rivers flow, how mountains range, what direction a highway is likely to go and other geographic or developmental challenges and opportunities.

"When I do my surveying, I like to do at night. If an area looks black, like Wyoming, Idaho or Montana, forget it. "To him, no lights means no customers. He knows that the customers and the money—like the lights—will be where the action is.

"There is no question about his ability to pick growth markets," says Pat Shivers, senior vice president, corporate controller, John Q. Hammons Hotels.

Rule 2: Know the Market

"When I first started in business, I was trying to sell a big shopping center in the middle of a cornfield. An old timer said to me, 'Son, you haven't run the BB test.' I asked what that was, and he said, 'Son, that's when you have to count the bellies on the block. There has to be a market for something, people to buy your product.'"

John Q. spends a lot of time now counting bellies.

HIS PREFERRED TYPE OF MARKET STUDY INCLUDES THE PERSON AT THE SHOESHINE STAND AND THE CAR RENTAL AGENT.

"I study the market conditions of one community and if I see something that works, I always wonder why wouldn't it work in another similar area. It usually does."

Veanne Stocking, regional vice president, John Q. Hammons Hotels, says that when she travels with him, he arrives in the airport and surrounds himself with the people who work there. His preferred type of market study includes the person at the shoeshine stand and the car rental agent. "Within minutes, he's surrounded by 20 people, and he's listening to their stories, asking them about how business is, what the area is like and what their own experiences are." He asks them where they think you should build a hotel. And it's a kind of research that works, because these are the people who know what's truly happening in the economy, who see and touch customers every day. They know whether things are good or bad, on the upswing or on the down slide. In John Q.'s book, these are people whose opinions count.

He creates a bond with people on airplanes, in restaurants, wherever he happens to be. The first question he asks is, "Where are you from?" Since he knows something about every location you can name, he can then mention something he knows about their hometown, thus developing an immediate rapport. Once his foot is in the door, he can find out why they're in town, and thus build his stockpile of information about where and why people go where they go.

He's insatiable for information, which means that his mailbox is loaded with information he's requested from chambers of commerce around the country. And he constantly clips magazine and newspaper articles that give him insight into communities, and into consumer trends.

He figures a clever person with 50 years' experience doesn't have to hire a study done. John Q. doesn't. He just uses common sense. He's been known to come back from lunch at his hotel across the street from corporate headquarters and say, "Do you know how many cars are in the parking lot at the hotel?" It's his barometer for how good business is.

When he sees a location he thinks meets his criteria, he digs a little deeper. Early on he began using a five-point approach for finding out whether a potential location was worth his time.

1. Evaluate economic conditions and the flow of money in the community.
2. Look at the history of the banks. Have they grown over time? What has the story been for the last 10 or 20 years.
3. Consider if the people in the city are conservative or aggressive in their savings habits.
4. Find out if the city's administration is progressive and favorable to business. Attitude is the most important factor in every city's potential.
5. Determine the quality of the schools in the community. As training grounds for the city, they shape the people who work in and influence the community.

Today, he doesn't describe what he does in such pinpoint terms, probably because by now it's simply second nature to him.

"HIS YEARS OF EXPERIENCE ARE WORTH MORE THAN ANY FEASABILITY STUDY."

"I get the ingredients. I look at their economy, whether they're growing or not, how many projects they've completed successfully, and how many are on the drawing board. I'll go in and ask a lot of questions of the city, and they don't know why the hell I'm asking, but I do. The first thing I want to know is what their operating budget is. What's their budget 10 years from now, and so forth. I just want to know how they're planning to do it. I can ask questions like that, and that plays into my reasons for why I want to build there."

Many people marvel that John does no formal market research for his hotels. Although the franchisors he works with generally require feasibility studies of some sort, John pulls off deals in spite of his lack of traditional research. His methods appear to be more seat-of-the-pants, but seem to be just as effective. His years of experience are worth more than any feasibility study.

Some of his methods include his running joke about how he judges how busy a road is: "I count the number of turtles that don't make it across the road," and "I talk to cab drivers."

What may look like magic to some, is really a lot of information processing going on invisibly in that steeltrap mind of his. He reads *The Wall Street Journal* and tracks trends. Talks to his contacts to get in on some ground-floor information. Keeps his ear to the ground. Looks for places where new roads are being built. Asks questions. When he decides to invest in a location, it's because he's learned enough about it to believe that it's not a big risk at all.

He also pays attention to trends, not by conducting market research, but by being observant. "Back in the early '80s, I could see that women were coming into the marketplace. On airplanes they were dressed in business attire, carrying their attache cases. They were in business, and I knew that to them security would be important. That's one reason I build atrium hotels."

Some of his tactics aren't quite as pure, but they get the job done nonetheless. "One time a long time ago, I walked up to the front desk at a competing hotel and asked, 'Was Dr. Martin here last night?' They looked at the book and said no, he wasn't registered. And I said, 'Were you full?' The guy said, 'Oh, yeah, we were full.' That's all I wanted. There was no Dr. Martin. I just needed to know if they were full. You never learn anything unless you've got your eyes open and you're dedicated to being studious."

But this can be a tricky enterprise. Once, his informal research backfired. "I called and asked for someone, and there was actually a person by that name staying at the hotel. When he answered the phone, I asked for 'Goose.' He said, 'Goose who.' I hung up." John Q.'s not squeamish about getting caught. He's determined to get the data he needs, and he's not shy about doing unconventional things to get it.

As the Highway Goes, So Goes Development

One thing John Q. follows closely is the country's highway infrastructure. Since he was a beneficiary of the early highway boom, he knows how that works.

"HE'S EXTRAORDINARILY 'TREND FORWARD.' PEOPLE CALL IT VISIONARY, BUT TO ME HE'S ALWAYS BEEN AHEAD OF HIS TIME."

"I look at the growth of the Interstate system like a tree. Going up the middle is the trunk, like I-49 going south to north from New Orleans. Then I look at the crossroads, the branches of the tree, like I-20, I-30, I-40 and I-44 crossing I-49. Where I see a city that is becoming an artery between the main branches, cities like Fayetteville, Arkansas, I know it will grow."

"I don't waste my time in a place that can't grow. I don't waste my time trying to figure out why something did not happen, or why it could happen. I just want to know it *has* happened. Then I can evaluate its potential after that because of my experiences."

Mark Snyder, senior vice president of Embassy Suites Hotels, says, "He's extraordinarily 'trend forward.' People call it visionary, but to me he's always been ahead of his time. He's got an intuition about these things that goes far beyond anything customer research could show us. He understands and he thinks about the customer. That's why his hotels turn out the way that they do."

Like David Sullivan in the early years at Holiday Inn, Snyder has experienced John Q.'s "trend forwardness" in some unexpected ways. He's had members of his team call and say, "Mark, I just drove past a site in Austin, and there's a piece of land there with a big 'Coming soon, Embassy Suites' sign on it. Do you know anything about it?" And when Snyder checks around, he discovers that John Q. has already decided to put the hotel there, without making an application or getting even a verbal commitment.

Steve Joyce, executive vice president, owner & franchise services, Marriott Hotels, reports that Hammons is infamous for his unexpected announcements. "At the opening of our Oklahoma City Renaissance, in the middle of our opening ceremony, he made an announcement that he was going to build an Embassy Suites down the street. It was a surprise to me and a surprise to the mayor. Afterward, John said, 'You know, Steve, the mayor was here; I just had to do it.'"

Unconventional as they are, John's tactics—some of which he keeps a bit closer to the chest—work. And if they don't, what's the worst thing that could happen? If he's a few years off his prediction and builds a hotel slightly prematurely, he has the money to wait things out. He's confident that eventually his gut instinct and his informal research will pay off.

The Evil Banker

More than one person has admitted that John out-thought them when it comes to sites. Mortgage banker Dan Meyer, formerly with the C. C. Fletcher Mortgage Company and Baldwin United Corporation, met John Q. in 1959, and over the years worked on about 40 long-term mortgage loans on hotels for him.

"John Q. had a wonderful relationship with C. C. Fletcher, who I worked with. When John's father died, John sort of took "Coach" (as he called him) on as a surrogate father. He would call C. C. every Saturday, and they would banter. John Q. would ask, 'What's the interest rate?' C. C. would tell him, for instance, that it was six percent. And John would want to borrow for 5 percent. This went on and on.

"When John would build hotels, we'd go in and appraise them, go into the markets and see what were the competitors' room rates, occupancy and so on. John would project in those days, let's say a $49 rate in his pro forma. The competition would be getting $42. So C. C. would say, 'No, John, you won't get that; the competition's only getting $42.' John would say, 'Sure I will,' And eventually, when inflation went up, and the rate would reach $60 or $80 a night, John would call C. C. and say, 'Remember when you told me I'd never get $42?'" This kind of friendly banter characterized their relationship, but C. C. wasn't the only one John would remind of his successes.

The Patience to Cut Red Tape

Former Holiday Inn and Promus Chairman Michael D. Rose says, "In terms of getting a hotel built, John is masterful, because he has the patience to work through a political process in all these communities. Where a lot of people would just throw their hands up and say 'I don't have time,' John takes the time, stays in contact, pursues the deal, negotiates every last detail of it. Therefore, he gives himself a much better chance of being successful with those convention hotels than other people."

Board member David Sullivan agrees. "He has an uncanny ability to deal with city, county, municipal governments. He meets the needs of the government while at the same time being able to satisfy his own needs from a financial standpoint. Not many

---

"POLITICS DON'T CONTROL THE ECONOMY, SUPPLY AND DEMAND DOES."

---

people can deal with the bureaucracy of government."

Although governments don't usually get in his way, sometimes things don't exactly turn out like he'd like. After all, every four years there's an election. When he's developed a relationship with one candidate, and another wins, it's sometimes back to the drawing board. But don't accuse John Q. of being political. As he says, "Politics don't control the economy; supply and demand does." He doesn't care if someone is Democratic or Republican, just as long as they know how to make a deal.

Rule 3: Build the Best Hotels

Five days a week (when he's in town), at about 11:30 a.m., you can find John Q. across the street from his office having lunch at his hotel, the University Plaza. Nine times out of ten, he's with Steve Minton, the architect who has spent the last 17 years making John Q.'s dreams come true. Dreams of hotels. Tall hotels. Hotels with visual impact. And with the little touches that turn an ordinary hotel into "another exceptional hotel by John Q. Hammons."

John Q. and Steve walk to the back of the restaurant, where there is a six-foot corner table, no tablecloth, set up. They're not looking for frills. Mr. Hammons goes around to sit at the back side of the table, where he can survey the property and "mind the store." He orders something light. Then he pulls out his yellow legal pad and his marker. And for the next hour, he talks hotel design.

"He's a very creative person," says Steve. He has big dreams, and he's always dreaming. I've never come to work wondering if I'll have enough to do that day. It's amazing that as much as we do, as much as we try, we just can't accomplish enough. He's always got new things on his mind."

Quality Sells

Part of the success of the Holiday Inn brand was its ubiquitousness. In a short time, the name Holiday Inn meant "hotel." Fast development, however, also meant that not all the hotels were built to last. To John Q.'s way of thinking, speed and economy sometimes spelled "cheap." It wasn't the kind of product he wanted to build. He wanted to build properties that were lasting and that met his guests' needs for years to come. He wanted to create centerpieces for the communities he served. He wanted to create something that served as a beautiful backdrop for great service. It wasn't all about making money, it was about creating a tangible dream.

"HE REALLY FEELS HE'S ON A MISSION TO TRY AND PROVIDE QUALITY LODGING IN ALL LOCATIONS, WHETHER THEY ARE SMALLER TOWNS OR BIGGERS TOWNS."

Quality facilities are designed for the long run, and Hammons wants each of his hotels to last. They're intended to be "the" community hotel, a "happening" place where locals will gather, hold their meetings, get married and be entertained, just as travelers will.

"He is one of the true characters of the business," says Steve Joyce of Marriott. "He is a very thoughtful man. He probably knows as much about real estate in this country as anybody does. There is not a street corner that you can talk about without him saying, 'Is that the one that has a gas station...I think I've got a piece of land there. Is that really where you want a hotel?'"

"He has a real sense of obligation about the business," says J. W. Marriott, Jr. "He's on a mission to provide quality lodging in all locations, whether they are smaller towns or bigger towns. His idea of quality lodging experience is a full-service hotel that's secure, where he can keep his guests safe and they have a great service experience. He's one of these guys who doesn't come in and out with fads. He believes what he believes, and he keeps moving ahead. Sometimes he falls out of fashion, but he always comes back because he just keeps doing what he's doing. He's been successful for 40-some years. There's no doubt that he'll keep going and being successful as long as he lives."

Each hotel under the John Q. Hammons umbrella welcomes guests when they arrive in their rooms following check-in. The letter announces Hammons' commitment to quality as well as to the well being of his guests.

To Our Guests

In ancient times there was a prayer for
"The Stranger within our gates"

Because this hotel is a human institution to serve people, and not solely a money making organization, we hope that God will grant you peace and rest while you are under our roof.

May this suite and hotel be your 'second' home. May those you love be near you in thoughts and dreams. Even though we may not get to know you, we hope that you will be comfortable and happy as if you were in your own house.

May the business that brought you our way prosper. May every call you make and every message you receive add to your joy. When you leave, may your journey be safe.

We are all travelers. From 'birth till death' we travel between the eternities. May these days be pleasant for you, profitable for society, helpful for those you meet, and a joy to those who know and love you best.

-Author Unknown-

He's not kidding about quality. Every one of his general managers knows it. And everyone on his design team.

"Mr. Hammons looks for the details," says project manager Marty McGahan. Marty was the project manager for Hammons' residence, and was then recruited to help build hotels. "He wants us to watch our costs; he wants to create projects that are a notch above our competition. Our guest rooms are often larger than the franchise brand requires, and we often install higher levels of finishes throughout the project too. An eye for the details is one of the ways Mr. Hammons stays ahead of his competition. He's become a great admirer of European-style hotel architecture and wants to incorporate this look into his newer hotel projects. Our challenge is to re-create this look on his tight project budget. European-style hotel architectural looks are a very expensive look to construct."

A Room with a View, Inside and Out

It's no wonder people call him a visionary; being able to see for long stretches is important to John Q. "I like a panoroma," he says. "And I like the command position you've got of your viewpoint. If you're in the valley, you can't see everything like that."

He likes natural beauty, and he brings that to his hotels whenever possible. Many of John Q.'s properties sit atop a hill, overlook a body of water or have a scenic view of woods and sunsets.

And, of course, there are the atriums that characterize not only his signature Plaza Hotels, but many of the other brands he's built.

No matter what John Q. Hammons development you visit, you're pretty certain to encounter a waterfall, a fountain, a lake, or some water-focused attraction. Whereas some people might say that the water engenders serenity or peace, to John Q. it means action. He has an affinity for water features. At one time, his hotels featured three-story-tall indoor waterfalls. Because of maintenance and noise issues, those have shrunk a bit to a more manageable size that can still bring a feeling of nature to the inside.

Coupled with great, quality construction is the outstanding service that is always a feature of a John Q. Hammons property.

"John was one of the first to recognize that quality paid off in the long run," says Mike Rose, chairman of Gaylord Entertainment.

Although Hammons made his fortune in Holiday Inn hotels, in the late '80s he began to invest more heavily in other, more upscale brands. Today, his portfolio includes brands known for quality, among them Marriott Hotels and Embassy Suites Hotels.

Mark Snyder of Embassy Suites has known Hammons for only two or three years, but he knows the man well. "Truly a golden thread that runs through all the conversations I have with Mr. Hammons is about quality and about ensuring that our older hotels remain top notch. He'll say, 'When are you gonna get rid of these older hotels? If you want me to help you replace some of them, I'll help you do it. Remember, Mark, in September they don't give the crown to grandma in Atlantic City (referring to the Miss America Pageant).'" He may not be politically correct, but he does know what he's talking about when it comes to keeping product fresh and "winning" in customers' eyes.

Tom Keltner, executive vice president of Hilton Hotels Corporation, says that at some points it's true the hotel business has been overbuilt, but that never deterred John. "John always said, 'The

---

"THE INDUSTRY'S NOT OVERBUILT, IT'S UNDERDEMOLISHED."

---

industry's not overbuilt, it's underdemolished.'" Hammons knows the marketplace, knows the customer and knows that the key to the future is in keeping the product like new. He doesn't stop building just because the economy is slow, or because money is hard to come by.

"I've always survived because I believe in quality. At that managers' conference where I told our people I intended to stay in the upscale, quality business, I told them I was going to put meeting space in our hotels. And that the meeting spaces will be big, like 10, 15 or even 40,000 square feet, because that's our insurance policy. I knew that the trends for big conventions like in Chicago, New York, Miami, San Francisco and L.A., Seattle, et cetera, were going to be a thing of the past because you can't afford to get there. I knew. I could see that coming. That's why I wanted to go into a region where I could be in the dominant position.

"I saved many hotels by doing that, because when the down times come, if you just have a hotel, you may have a pretty good piece of real estate but your budget's in the discount bin, and you don't have anything to offer. I've got something to offer. Keep your properties up and go upscale. Put that convention center there and you can still be in business having your meetings and things like that."

He believes if he builds it right, and he gives people what they want, they'll buy.

Steve Minton, corporate architect, explains John's preferences: "He really loves doing quality projects whether it's a Marriott or an Embassy Suites. We do smaller projects once in awhile, but those aren't as fun for him. The smaller ones can be moneymakers, and that's great, but they're not projects that he's going to get very excited about. Because when he walks into a hotel, he wants to see that atrium with the waterfall and the skylights and all the trees. There are definitely occasions when we could spend less money and still have a similar product, and still do good business, but he demands we do something extra special. If he was just in this to do business, he'd make a business decision and say, save the cost. He's in it for the excitement of creating the project."

Jim Anderson, president of the Springfield Area Chamber of Commerce, before approaching John with a proposal to underwrite a portion of the Chamber's new Enterprise center, suggested that the architect include a fountain out front. A clever strategic move on Anderson's part. How much the presence of the fountain contributed to John's decision to be involved in the project, we may never know.

"HE'S IN IT FOR THE EXCITEMENT OF CREATING THE PROJECT."

David Sullivan jokingly suggests he's tried that trick himself: "I was proposing that the public company agree to make a contribution to the University of Memphis Hospitality School that Kemmons Wilson created. John Q. was ill and wasn't at the board meeting where this was presented. But I told the board, "Hey, we'll be happy to name a fountain after him." Someone said, "You've got a fountain down there?" I said, "Yeah, it's just a water fountain, but I'll put John Q.'s name on it."

His penchant for fountains may be a source of fun for onlookers, but you can't deny that John has a knack for spotting what will attract guests. His hotels have track records that stand on their own, proof that John Q. knows what sells.

Rule 4: Stay in Tune with Guests

The fourth rule of development for John Q. is that he stays in touch with guests' needs. He hires great people to run the hotels, and he's very conscious of how guests' desires change. In an age where it's difficult to find good employees, he seems to have his pick. How? "We grow 'em and we steal 'em," he says. On one trip, Veanne Stocking, regional vice president, recalls that John Q. was in town to survey a new property he was building. He was staying at a competitor's hotel. "He called the hotel, and had the van driver pick him up at the airport and take him to the site of his new property. Throughout the drive, John Q. talked with the man and liked him. He told the guy that when the new hotel opened, he wanted him to be the head bellman. About a year later, when the hotel was ready to open, John Q. found him and hired him for that job. He's a man of his word."

Stephen Marshall, the general manager at The Chateau, is another Hammons find. He was working for a four-star hotel when someone told him that John Q. was looking for someone to run the new property. "The next day, I was on an airplane, and I saw a big four-color ad in the flight magazine for John Q. Hammons Hotels. I didn't think much more about it, but about a month later I got a call, this time from Mr. Hammons himself." Needless to say, Stephen was convinced.

Rule 5: Control Costs

The last factor in making John Q. successful is that he's cost conscious. "We always paid our mortgage first," says Frank James, former regional vice president.

With his eye for quality and devotion to building hotels that are differentiated from the market, you'd think that John Q. might be less concerned with costs. He loves the creation process and adores a beautiful product. But he grew up in the Depression, and his regard for money was shaped by his family's financial tragedy. And he worked as a cost accountant on the Alaska Highway. The man who confidently risks millions on unproven markets also believes that there's no reason to waste paper clips. Board member David Sullivan laughs. "We have a board dinner, and it just kills him if they serve steak. I'm not kidding you. He'll say, 'We can't afford this. Next time we're having hamburgers.'"

He's got to keep costs down to make his projections come true. Thanks to his photographic memory, no financial detail goes unnoticed. And no design detail, either. The balancing act his team has to play is keeping the quality up and the costs down.

"REVENUE HIDES A LOT OF THINGS. WHEN THINGS GET TOUGH, YOU'LL FIND OUT WHICH MANAGERS HAVE BEEN SWIMMING NAKED."

Building is one side of the cost-control equation. Operations is the other. He routinely looks at the performance of every hotel, calling a general manager to ask about a dip in profits or an occupancy downturn. And there's always a clear directive to keep costs under control.

His wisdom: "Revenue hides a lot of things. When things get tough, you'll find out which managers are swimming naked."

From time to time, John Q. lights a fire under everyone. Here's a memo he wrote in August 2000.

THEY CALL HIM JOHN Q.

To: All General Managers
From: John Q. Hammons

This subject is **IMPORTANT!!** What happened to our business during the month of July? Many of our hotels were caught sleeping at the wheel by the 4th of July holiday, and this was very disappointing!

Since ringing in the New Year, everyone has had access to a July calendar for business planning purposes. It's a well-known fact that whenever a holiday falls in the middle of the week, serious trouble lies ahead. While the holidays may be great fun for the masses, they affect many business' livelihood — and particular hotels!

I've been in the hotel business for over 40 years, and many of you have also been around for a number of years. We will always experience the same 'holiday cycles' year after year, so why weren't you alert to the business downturn, which historically takes place during these times?

The first six months we sailed along with well over $1.4 million at the NOI level, and then July comes along and we're back to square one. We continue to approve recommendations for salary increases, bonuses and advancements when requested. And then a month like July comes around, and we question not only your attention to detail but also the wisdom of our decision to reward poor management judgment.

Everyone knows how hard we have all worked to make our company successful. It is your company, and we depend on your performance. We can't continue to accept lack of planning and preparation any more. If you had anticipated the 4th of July holiday weeks in advance, a lot of expense could have been avoided.

Will you please help us? We need your teamwork. We need the experience of your many years in the hotel business.

Leave the sleeping to our guests!

When he calls the front desk at one of his hotels at 11 o'clock at night to ask what the occupancy is, John Q. is minding the store.

He expects nothing less of the people he's given the responsibility for protecting his assets.

Quality Rubs Off

Over the years, John Q. and Kemmon Wilson have remained linked through friendship. In 2002, John Q. had a personal visit with Kemmons in Memphis, and took a look at the Kemmons Wilson Hospitality School that opened at the University of Memphis. Wilson intends the school to be a hands-on learning experience for students who want to make a career of hotel management.

As they toured the hotel facility, John Q. asked all the right questions. "So, how many square feet you have in this ballroom, 14,000?" Kemmons said yes, that was about right. With a twinkle in his eye, John Q. said, "Kemmons, it looks like you spent more money on this one than you used to."

"Well, John, I've been trying to live up to your standards," Wilson laughed.

Spreading the News

Once he's decided a hotel is going to be built, that's all she wrote, because dealing with John Q. is like dealing with the Barnum and Bailey of the lodging industry. He announces his new deals when and where he feels like it, whether the franchise organization has blessed the project or not, whether the city fathers have come to the table, whether he has money in the bank. John Q. is the ultimate PR man, who carries pocket-size directories to give away to anyone who will take one. On airplanes, he tells people who he is. He wants to buy four-color ads in big publications, even when his marketing budget doesn't call for it. He calls the PR departments of companies like Hilton Hotels and pursues them for releases on his developments. He touts his hotels every chance he gets. And it's not bragging. It's fact. They are exceptional hotels.

When Walter Cronkite complimented The Chateau as ranking at the top of the hotels he'd seen around the world, to John Q. that was just an opening to ask more: "Did you see any of the suites? Do you see the view? I've got some postcards..."

You might mistake the developer for a salesman. You might be right.

That's because it's easy for John Q. to sell something he believes in. As Mark Snyder of Embassy Suites says, "When I drive up to one of his hotels, I get the sense that what he has created is the centerpiece of the community. He wants the community to feel like this is their hotel. Whether it's the weddings on the weekend, restaurants, Chamber of Commerce meeting, the community will gravitate toward this hotel. You just don't have developers who think that way. They think about it as an asset, as bricks and mortar; they think about it from the bottom line and the return standpoint. Mr. Hammons, of course, thinks about it that way as well, but he's building for a bigger cause. He's got a bigger idea. He wants to be a part of that city. And he's done that in every location he's gone to."

6

How Does He Do the Deal?

In the first half of his life, when John Q. regularly played Monopoly with his buddies, he wasn't just having a good time. He was studying, learning how to read people, learning to concentrate and to recognize what made for a good deal. Years later, it's stood him in good stead. What he learned in fun he applies in work, using his skill to make deals that most people would die for.

In a conversation with Mr. and Mrs. Hammons, associate John Fulton, asked John Q., "I know you built a hotel empire, but I've got to know how you play Monopoly." John Q. looked at him and said, "All I can tell you is when I sit down, I don't aim to lose." From all accounts, he seldom does lose, in Monopoly or in life.

Anyone who knows John Q. for more than about five minutes can tell that he's all about "the deal." That's what gets his adrenaline racing, and it's what keeps him excited about life. There's always a deal—or twenty—brewing.

Defining how he does what he does is like trying to hold a fistful of Jell-O. His deals change shape before your eyes. Because every project is different, he invents it as he goes along. It's a process of reading the players and figuring out how to create a win-win. Those who watch him say they can't replicate the process, but they have gleaned some of the principles that guide his approach.

The Science and Art of Winning

"If it's a good deal, it'll be there today and probably tomorrow. If it's a bad deal, it'll be there for a lot longer," he says.

Hammons' common sense theory is that you have to buy the property right, so that you can build the property right, then operate it right so that eventually you'll be able to sell it right. Many people interpret "right" to mean cheap: buy the land cheap, build it cheap, operate it cheap. That's not what John Q. means. He means the property has to be in the best location, you have to pay a fair price for the property; you have to build a good property – not a cheap property - and you have to run it with a quality operation so that when you get ready to sell it, you can get top dollar for it. It's paid off for him all through the years.

Being the most prolific independent hotel developer in the country is a distinction John Q. has earned through his ability to make deals by using OPM (other people's money) and by doing deals that are favorable to both sides. "If you do a deal that's not good for both participants, it will come back to bite you," says Hammons.

Mickey Powell should know. He's sat on both sides of the table from Mr. Hammons, as a developer with Hilton Hotels, and as a member of the John Q. Hammons development team. "His approach is to enter negotiations from an absolute position of power without being a Douglas MacArthur. He's able to go in really politely and get his point across, and let the historical track record speak for itself."

Other People's Money

What's his favorite way to make a deal? Find a way to use other people's money. And he has the wherewithal to do that. "Never borrow more than you can afford to pay back," says John Q.

He has a collection of favorite sayings that he loves to share with his friends, employees, associates, strangers...in fact, just about anyone with whom he comes in contact. He used to send out cards printed with them. One that he particularly likes is called **The Developer's Creed in a Period of Double-Digit Inflation:**
A dollar borrowed is a dollar earned.
A dollar refinanced is a dollar saved.
A dollar repaid is a dollar lost forever!
　　*Circulated at the request of John Q. Hammons

Author Unknown

Motivation Is Everything

"I want to know why a guy's going to sell. There's always a motivation to sell, and I have to know those reasons. I find that out by taking the conversation in different directions. I evaluate what he does; who he's associated with. I'm always thinking."

Hammons tells about a piece of land he bought for $650,000. He has an idea to build a corporate retreat there. "You know what's cooking? They're already asking me if I'll take a million dollars for it. When I get it up to $1.5 million I might let 'em have it. I guess that earmarks who I am. I take a gamble to do a deal, but if I think the gamble is not worth all the effort, what's wrong with making some money? I've done nothing except have my man go up and walk around it. And that's a true story."

It's not an uncommon occurrence in John Q.'s business for him to fund a hotel with a real estate deal. Like in Tulsa, where he bought a piece of land for $6.7 million. He sold five acres at a profit, and had plans to sell all but the amount of land he needs to build a hotel. At that point, he says, "The site will be free."

One thing's for sure: You never tell John Q. he can't do something.

When he finally decided the time was right to build The Chateau on the Lake near Branson, "The banks thought I was over the edge and gone. Put a hotel like that in Branson territory? You're out of your mind. So when we finished we had $60 million in cash in it and I couldn't get a loan. So I went ahead and opened. Four months later, I got a loan for $35 million. Just like that."

Hobby Airport Beckons

Some years back, Hobby Airport in Houston was closed for a time. Then, John Q. got wind that it might reopen. When he heard that Southwest Airlines was planning to go into Hobby Airport, that was the clincher. "I figured that was a star in the East, and I might as well pay attention." He became determined to get in on the ground floor with a hotel. He saw a piece of land that he figured was perfect, except for one thing: It wasn't for sale.

One of the groups involved was a church that had its building on one part of the site, and also had an empty parcel that it wasn't using. He made an offer to buy a portion of the property. They declined because they had concerns about how a hotel might affect the environment around the church. John Q. thought long and hard, using his theory about knowing why a person would want to sell. He came up with the magic question: "What's your mortgage on the church?" The pastor replied about a million dollars. "I'll pay it," said John Q. "The pastor put down his Bible and started listening."

And today, there is a Marriott Hotel on that site, serving the customers of Southwest Airlines and Hobby Airport.

Patience Versus Action

Some might say that John Q. is impatient because he's always pushing to get projects up and running, and always anxious to get

---

HE DOESN'T MAKE DECISIONS ON OTHER PEOPLE'S TIMETABLES.

---

hotels built. But his history of buying land and then waiting decades to develop it seems to prove that he's actually a very patient man.

And when it comes to making decisions, he doesn't make decisions on other people's timetables.

He's a guy who can do what he says he can do. As developer and friend Mickey Powell says, "He's not someone who has to call back and check with somebody before he can say yes. You're not dealing with a developer that goes, 'Yes, I'll build that hotel,' and then has to spend 18 months or two years trying to find financing or trying to find a general contractor to build it. You're dealing with a guy that can go do what he says he can do. When I worked for him that was one of his strong points that I realized and recognized very quickly. I'd go to represent Mr. Hammons in Des Moines or Omaha or anywhere, and when I sat down to talk to the city or the mayor or to a realtor and told them who I worked for, in 90 percent of the cases they'd heard of Mr. Hammons. In the few cases that they hadn't, I gave them contacts that they visited with. They quickly realized that they were dealing with someone that could do what he said he was going to do."

One reason he's known is because he's the only one in the country dropping $30 million or so in secondary communities. Cities are hungry for development; Hammons has the clout, the wherewithal and the history to make it happen. He's a man who has put skylines in towns that would never have had one if not for him. In regional markets especially, the quality of his products is well established. What more could a city want in a partner?

Check Your Ego at the Door

When John Q. is looking to make a deal, he says there's one rule he follows: "Never let your ego outdistance your judgment. You've got to keep your ego in check." It's a bit hard to believe that John Q. can practice that, because he clearly has a healthy ego. "Everyone who's successful has an ego, they have to," he says.

John Q. was featured in an article once as saying, "A lot of people may think I have an ego. I don't think I do. I don't know. I just do business and work hard."

Considering how many things are named for him, it does make one wonder about the size of that ego. Then again, maybe it's not his ego that makes him do it; maybe it's his marketing savvy.

Frank James was the first Winegardner & Hammons hotel general manager. He helped build the company, working with John Q. from 1964 until Frank retired in 1990. He explains one theory of how James Quentin Hammons became John Q.

"John actually was born James Quentin Hammons, and the family and friends called him Quentin. When he started his development work, though, he would go into towns to do his own type of feasibility study. That meant talking to bellmen, taxi drivers, all the regular people. When he'd approach the city administrators, or the banks, he would never introduce himself. He would just say, 'I'm John Q.,' to represent John Q. Public. He didn't want anyone to know who he was, because he felt that way he maintained an edge. So, everyone began calling him John Q."

One of the strongest assets John Q. has is his name; as a marketing tool, a development lever, a borrowing weight. Those are just a few reasons John Q. is all about preserving and propagating his good name. After all, there have been times when that's all he had, and other times when his good name alone was sufficient to seal a deal.

James explains: "At one point, we were building a restaurant on top of a hotel, and we were considering what to name it. I suggested we call it John Q.'s. John didn't like that, because he was very protective of his name, and he was concerned about putting

---

"IN THE OLD DAYS, HE USED TO APPROACH CITIES. NOW THEY APPROACH HIM."

---

his name on something that might not be highly successful. He said, 'But Frank, what if the food is bad or something.' I said, 'Don't be silly. It will be very high quality and a big success.' He reluctantly let us name the restaurant after him.

"Later, John Q. began to realize that having people recognize his name was a development advantage. When he went into a city to pursue a development deal, if the bankers and city officials had heard his name and knew his reputation, it smoothed the way. Over time, his name packed power. In the old days, he used to approach cities. Now, they approach him."

That's because backing up the John Q. Hammons name are qualities that endear bankers, guests, communities and employees to his properties: A great product, outstanding service, financial success and community involvement.

Leveraging His Name

Taking his good name, John Q. can go into a city and expect that his reputation preceeds him. His approach then is to go to a city where he intends to build and offer a proposal that might sound like this:

"Listen, here's what I'll do: I'll take this city block that you have down here, and you're going to lease it to me for a $1 a year or sell it to me for a $1. I'll build you a 250-room, nine-story atrium hotel with glass elevators, waterfalls, two restaurants, two lounges, and 15,000 square feet of meeting space. You're going to build a parking deck behind it for me and lease that to me for so much. Now if you all don't want to do this, I understand. It's your property, and it's your city. But I'm going from here to Lincoln, Nebraska. I can do four projects this year at $25 million a project, and it really makes no difference to me whether I do it here or in Lincoln. They're both state capitals, they both have interstates, both have airports and I'm prepared to go to the next place over here. You just let me know what you want to do."

According to people who have been there, that's when the city council or the mayor would flinch from what they could tell is a man telling the truth. Whereas some developers would come hat in hand to beg for permission to do a deal, John Q. merely puts his offer out there and says take it or leave it.

It's not unusual that within a day or so, a mayor will call and say, "Mr. Hammons, I think we're going to be able to deliver that land to you up there for a dollar after all."

"DON'T EVER SIT DOWN TO A NEGOTIATING TABLE THAT YOU'RE NOT PREPARED TO GET UP AND WALK AWAY FROM."

Acting Pays Off

College theater productions were good training ground for John Q., who is still using his acting skills. Suffice it to say that when he sits down at a negotiating table, he relies on all the skills he's been honing for life.

"Two of the hardest things to do are to buy something that Mr. Hammons owns, because he doesn't need to sell it, and to loan him money, because he doesn't need it," says Powell. "He's always told me, 'Don't ever sit down to a negotiating table that you're not prepared to get up and walk away from.'"

One group was shocked when John Q. decided to break a multi-million dollar deal over a $35 fee that he believed was incorrectly charged to his side of the contract. He simply walked away from the table. Lawyers quickly managed to adjust the paperwork, and John Q. got the deal the way he wanted it—minus the $35 fee. Then again, maybe he's not acting. Maybe he simply never gets so attached to a deal that he can't break loose over something that's not his way, no matter how insignificant or inconsequential the detail may be.

It's amazing how many people cave. It may be that he's a good actor who hides his ardor for a deal. Or that he doesn't get emotionally attached to a deal. But those who have seen him in action know that if he walks away, he will eventually find a way to make a sweeter deal, and likely, a highly visible comeback.

A Mind Made for Deals

His "I'm-just-a-country-boy-from-Missouri" demeanor sometimes belies the incredibly savvy businessman he is. "I got a new pair of overalls to wear to the franchise meeting," he's likely to joke to a friend. Don't be fooled. His mind is a state-of-the-art computer.

He has a photographic memory, and can recite for you how much he paid for land and how much he spent on a hotel, no matter how many years ago it was. This talent he considers a blessing and a curse, because his mind is crammed with so many details that he can never forget.

According to Sales and Marketing Vice President Scott Tarwater, John Q. would rather read a profit-and-loss statement than a good novel. His negotiating skills are legendary, because he can and will walk away from any deal.

Every conversation is punctuated with comments about Highway-this, and Interstate-that. He can draw the entire Interstate system on a yellow legal pad. And it's possible he may be able to tell you where the fire hydrants are located and what color the bus bench is in front of a drugstore in Boise. "Never bet with him on geography," says Terry Bichsel, former senior vice president of operations. "He knows absolutely every highway, every intersection, every good piece of real estate in the country."

Then there's that visionary thing again. Jacquie Dowdy, his personal finance advisor, says he can see things no one else can. She laughs as she tells this story: "We were going to put a Burger Station on a lot, and he had me drive out there with him to look at it. I was driving along, and he suddenly said, 'Jacquie, you're driving through the middle of the building.' And I said, 'I'm sorry, I can't see it!'"

John Q. can make anything seem real. And if you're in a conversation with him that lasts more than two minutes, you're sure to hear him say with sincerity and a serious demeanor, "Now that's a true story," his way of underlining the importance of what he's just said.

Hello, John?

Anyone who keeps multiple deals going simultaneously needs a lifeline. For John, it's the phone. Ask someone where John is at any given moment, and they'll probably say, "On the phone."

Jim McCauley, former executive director of the International Association of Holiday Inn (IAHI) franchise group, was on the receiving end of many of John's calls. "One time I got a call from John and I said, 'Hey, John, where are you?' He said, 'I'm in an airport.' I said, 'What city?' and he said, 'I don't know. I was on a plane to Philadelphia, and when it stopped I got off to use the phone.'"

His phone "addiction" has drawn jokes and ribbing from friends and colleagues. Someone once described John Q. walking by a bank of phones in an airport. "It's like an addict walking by a bowl of Quaaludes!"

When John served on the board of IAHI, one of the members, Ralph Deckelbaum, came into the meeting carrying his briefcase. He placed his briefcase on the table, and sat down. The meeting commenced. After about 20 minutes, the briefcase began to ring. This being well before the advent of cell phones, Ralph looked puzzled. Then he got up and opened the briefcase, reached in and took out a phone—cord and all—and answered, "Hello? Oh, John, it's for you."

"When we'd do conferences or meetings, I would always run into John down in the lobby using the phone," says John Nowak, director of meetings and special events for Hilton Hotels. "I'd say, 'Hi, Mr. Hammons, what are you doing?' and he'd say, 'Minding the store.'"

Some people claim he uses the lobby phone because he's frugal: he's reluctant to use the phone in his hotel room because he doesn't want to pay the surcharge. More important, though, is the comment he made to Nowak about minding the store. By standing in the lobby, he can keep an eye on what's happening in the hotel. He's been known to stand in an empty lobby and call the front desk to ask, "How's your business?" Woe to the front desk person who claims business is good when it's not, because John Q. will hang up the phone, walk over and say, "Hey, this place is dead. Where's all that occupancy?"

Lonnie Funk, former executive vice president of operations, says, "He has tremendous intuition. He can be in a property for just a minute and read the morale, the occupancy. It's uncanny, almost scary."

John Q. could have invented the term "multitasking." In fact, one general manager remembers that before cordless phones, he used to make special arrangements for John Q. when he was visiting. "We had to make sure we had an extra long phone cord so that John Q. could stretch the phone out to the pool. He would sit there in his slacks, take off his shirt and work on his tan while he did deals on the phone."

Frank James says that John's legendary photographic memory comes in handy for his phone habit. "He memorized about 300 phone numbers, and he'd just jot the name, phone number and topic on a legal pad, and he'd be off and running." Of course, in recent years, he also relies heavily on the people in his office to deal with details. He often calls receptionist Rose Rear with cryptic instructions: "Get that guy at the 405 area code for me," or "Get that guy in Texas." "He can remember an area code from 15 years ago," says Rose. An ability to read minds is a definite advan-

---

"I RUN FASTER THAN MOST PEOPLE SEE."

---

tage when you work for John Q. His mind works so fast, he's always two steps ahead of everyone. He's got so much information computing in his head, it's hard for us mortals to follow his line of thought. "I run faster than most people can see," he says. And you get the definite impression he's not exaggerating a bit.

His favorite picture of himself shows him phone in hand. At the airport, between flights, you can always find him talking business. You might think that the invention of the cell phone would be a godsend to John, right? Nope. He doesn't have the time to worry with the batteries, and all that. He's got his 300 most important phone numbers in his head, and deals are waiting to be made. So, like the ladies in Vegas who operate three slots at a time, he still uses pay phones, monopolizing a bank of phones, keeping several conversations going at once. In fact, a friend (John Cleghorn) once sent him for his birthday a real, full-size telephone booth inscribed with "John Q. Hammons' Private Phone." He installed it on his patio.

More than once John has missed flights because of phone calls that had to be made, or because he was on an excursion to check out potential development. One of his business associates, Lee McLean, tells of a time they had to change planes in Denver. "Hammons was always carrying a camera to take pictures of land. He was taking pictures in the Denver airport terminal, and our plane was about to take off. The flight attendant asked me, 'Where's your buddy? We've got to go.' I said, 'Well, okay, let's go.' And we did. Left him there. When we arrived at our destination, I went to my hotel and went to bed. About 11 or 12 o'clock, I get a call from John. 'You ran off and left me in Denver!' he said. And I asked him where he was. He said 'I'm in Denver and can't get a plane.' But about five minutes later he knocked on the door and we had a good laugh. He had just gotten busy and forgotten about the flight."

Speed's Essential

Some 20 years ago, Hammons was doing lots of real estate transactions and his assistant, Jan Robbins, had her real estate license and had worked for several excellent attorneys prior to joining John Q. When he was working on a deal, he loved to say to the people he was working with, 'Well, I'm going to let you talk to my half-assed attorney.' Having great respect for the legal field, Jan would wince. Hammons is always looking to get a deal done as fast as possible. Some attorneys are known for taking hours and hours and dragging you through every nitpicking thing. He calls them "deal-breakers." Mr. Hammons' modus operandi has always been find the site, this is what I'll pay and I'll close tomorrow. He wants a deal done now. He will say, "So what if there's a hair on it? Shave it and move on." No deal ever happens fast enough for him.

Playing the Odds

Life for John is a perpetual Monopoly game. Every day, he takes a turn around the board, talking with the various cities in which he hopes to make a deal. He keeps multiple deals going because he figures if he announces 20 projects, 10 will get done. His phone rings off the wall, and he's constantly jumping on an airplane. Even though he's not a gambler, he's clearly playing the odds. And besides, it's a great way to stay in shape. "I stay busy, stay away from cigarettes and alcohol. For fitness, I run through airports."

7

Leading the Troops

The movie "Patton" portrays U. S. General George S. Patton lecturing troops about how they must perform to defeat the enemy. Patton stands tall, rigid, exuding strength and pride. No one has a doubt that he will lead them to victory. He's driven, visionary and intent upon maintaining his in-charge persona. He looks people dead straight in the eye. Patton would, perhaps, have made a good developer.

There are parallels with John Q., a man who also sees himself as a leader of troops, a person who must maintain a tough persona. He appreciates the value of history and has studied leaders like Patton. He, too, believes in keeping some distance between himself and his troops, in challenging people to new heights rather than coaxing them along. As a man who loves to teach, he proffers lessons and expects people to learn. And rather than using the more tolerant form of management popular in recent years, he believes that he can inspire people to perform by constantly setting the bar higher. He seems to defy all modern management principles. Yet his company excels in almost every performance measure.

It's not warm and fuzzy by any means, but somehow it works. John Q. is a one-man show, but he's managed to get a lot of people on board with him. They support his quality, they carry out his goals, they deliver the results he wants. And while they're at it, they're proud of what they do.

J. W. Marriott, Jr., of Marriott Hotels, once told him, "The pride that you and your associates have is reflected in your company's tremendous culture."

Old-Fashioned Leadership, Modern Victories

In an age when most companies are struggling to maintain employees for two years, John Q.'s organization is out of the ordinary. Take an average of the number of years his team has been with him, and you'll undoubtedly be surprised. At head-quarters, most people's tenure with the company is in double digits. (And a lot of those who leave find their way back. It's hard to leave a kingdom where you get to work on some of the most desirable projects in the country.)

Finding associates who will run great hotels is no easy task, but John Q. seems to have the knack. Where does he get great people? He uses that "grow 'em and steal 'em" tactic. He's really not kidding when he uses that phrase. He knows how important good people are. "No hotel is better than its management," he says, so when he sees someone he likes, he finds a way to make them a part of his John Q. Hammons family.

Ask people how they came to work for John Q., and most of the time, you'll hear how he recruited them away from other compa-nies. Like the van driver he stole from a competitor a year before John Q.'s hotel even opened.

Of course, giving someone the chance to work for the best game in town is usually a pretty easy sell. John Q.'s reputation alone is a draw. When people go into the hotel business, they find out pretty quickly who the players are. John Q. is certainly at the head

---

"BEING A VISIONARY DOESN'T MEAN MUCH UNLESS YOU'RE WILLING TO STEP UP AND TAKE ACTION."

---

of the list. It's energizing—though sometimes exhausting—to work for a man who constantly makes things happen; who has the financial wherewithal and the personal stamina to keep things moving fast. One of the things that attracts people to John Q. is the fact that there's always something happening...in a big way.

They say at John Q. Hammons they get to work on projects they could never get to do at other companies.

"Being visionary doesn't mean much unless you're willing to step up and take action," says Regional Vice President Bob Niehaus. "John Q. steps up."

When he interviews people, he tells them some of the things he sees in the industry, as if he's teaching them something they don't know, and he'll ask them for a response. He's not trying to educate them on the trends, he just wants to see how they respond, what they're composed of, and how they're absorbing material about the hotel industry. He's interested in how people interpret information and make decisions.

Regional Vice President Tom Harwell says John Q. has a singular way of making people feel at ease. He just talks to people, with no hint that he's a powerful millionaire and they're not. As far as John Q. is concerned, everyone's opinion counts.

And his selection process is a bit unusual, too. "If I was going to hire a general manager and I couldn't get my bags in his trunk because it was full of sporting regalia, he wasn't the person for the job."

Strategic Versus Tactical

You won't find a strategic plan written out in John Q.'s office. It's all in his head. He doesn't share it, and, frankly, he probably doesn't believe that anyone needs to know it but him. He definitely believes that the right and left hand shouldn't know everything. That philosophy comes from hard-learned experience.

His view of running hotels, however, is a completely different issue; it's an open book. John Q. doesn't expect anyone to read his mind when it comes to his expectations of his hotels. He speaks clearly of what he wants. Talk to any of his managers and they can recite verbatim what he expects them to achieve in their hotels. John Q. knows how to get the word out. Quality first. Satisfy guests. Mind the store.

In the 1970s, he personally supervised every general manager, a method that insured every one of his hotels mirrored his philosophy. Even now, he tries to meet every new General Manager when he or she is hired. When John Q. comes into contact with anyone associated with his company, he takes the opportunity to make his feelings about quality and costs clear. To this day, there's little doubt that people understand his approach to business.

His general manager's creed, assembled by Lonnie Funk from John Q. Hammons' letters to the field over the years, tells it all.

GENERAL MANAGER'S CREED
Manages by walking around
Inspects what the guest expects
Demands outstanding guest service
Pays attention to the front desk
Provides excellent PBX service
Expects superior food and beverage quality
Profound interest in the welfare of the guest

Talks to the customers
Personally enjoys serving the guest
Hands-on manager
Manages by example
Participates in hiring and training
Motivates employee performance
Initiates effective communication
Open, honest and up-front with employees
Adheres to JQH employee manual policies
Actively concerned about employee safety
Perseveres through adversity
Stays positive and upbeat
Dedicated and hard-working leader
Takes pride in staff development
Watches the store
Protects and maintains the assets
Recognizes the hotel's role in the community
Demands cleanliness, cleanliness, cleanliness
Keeps the thieves at bay
Maintains a credible business behavior
Integrity is beyond reproach
Active hotel industry leader
Runs the hotel like an owner
Motivated by the P&L
Forecasts into the future
Knows what the competition is doing
Finds new markets
Leads the sales effort
Maximizes revenue opportunities
Practices yield management
Adheres to established labor standards
Challenges and questions everything
Enforces credit policies
Manages the accounts receivable
Maximizes NOI potential

John Q. doesn't need a mission statement and a communications plan. Like other great leaders, he tells stories—repeatedly. They travel throughout the company so that just about everyone can tell the folklore of the John Q. Hammons empire.

Who's Who?

Titles mean nothing to John Q., nor do positions. The people on his team are accustomed to filling multiple roles. He sees his own role as one of balancing whoever is in charge of his operations. If they are interested in costs, he becomes more interested in customer satisfaction and quality. If they tune in to marketing, he gets into cost control. And if they take an interest in development...hold everything. That sandbox is reserved for John Q. It's hard to imagine being second in command under John Q., because he's single-minded when it comes to how he thinks things should be run. But the truth is, he's happiest when he can leave all those other subjects to someone else and stay focused on what he loves best: doing the deal.

When he needs an answer, forget hierarchy and chain of command. John Q. prefers to talk directly to the people who know what he needs to know, and he actively seeks contact with people throughout his organization. Today, he may have team members whose titles are "regional vice president," but when he wants to know how the guests like the hotel, he'll stop a housekeeper in the hall or a bellman on an elevator.

Stephen Marshall, general manager of The Chateau on the Lake, says John Q. will sometimes call the hotel and ask for Jane, the night auditor. "The person who answers the phone might recognize his voice, and they'll ring me to say Mr. Hammons is on the line. I'll pick up, and he'll politely chat with me for a minute and then explain that he'd like to talk to Jane."

Teaching Is His Second Love

Those who can, do; those who can't teach. If ever anyone disproved that adage, it's John Q. He started out as a teacher, he has accomplished more than most people could in several lifetimes, yet he continues to teach. In fact, throughout his company, people describe him as a mentor.

As Bob Fugazi, regional vice president, says, "He communicates by telling stories. Great leaders communicate by telling a story and by having other people be able to visualize their vision."

"HE'S TOUGH ENOUGH TO LEAD, SOFT ENOUGH TO TEACH."

"I like to see people advance and mature and learn, and then do something with their learning," says John Q.

"He's tough enough to lead, soft enough to teach," says regional vice president Bill Mead. "What I learn from him is worth more than compensation," he says. "People save his letters and memos because they're so full of good advice." Not only do his employees save his memos, so do his friends, associates, acquaintances.

Bill Killian says John Q. has had more influence on his life than anyone besides his own father. "He has never let me get ahead of myself," says Killian. John Q. teaches, he says, by asking questions.

"Still today he's very much a teacher," says Veanne Stocking, regional vice president. "In every conversation he has, he gathers information about how he can help the other person grow."

Of course, John Q. isn't going to tell all of his secrets. In 1995, Bill Mead asked John Q. to teach him how to do deals the way he did.

"I'll teach you one of these days," Hammons said. Mead is still waiting for that lesson.

A Day's Pay for a Day's Work

His management style is old-fashioned: He believes in hard work and loyalty, honesty and integrity.

In 1982 management guru Ken Blanchard wrote a best-seller entitled *The One-Minute Manager.* John Q.'s management style probably doesn't mirror Blanchard's theory, but you can be sure that the "one minute" part is the foundation of his style. He has little time for anything but straight-to-the-point business.

When John Q. thinks someone has missed the boat, he may send a memo and carbon copy a long list of people such as the President of the United States to emphasize the size of the error!

"MOST OF THE TIME HE ALREADY KNOWS THE ANSWERS TO THE QUESTIONS HE ASKS. HE JUST WANTS TO BE SURE YOU KNOW THEM, TOO."

In the early days of The Chateau at the Lake, he was in heated discussions with his team about whether they should keep The Chateau open year-round. Several factors could contribute to the concept of closing it, because business tended to drop off and inclement weather in Branson can potentially make the road to The Chateau impassable. At the same time, closing it contributed to difficulty in hiring employees, and increased cost for opening and closing. Hammons sent the following note to his team:

For your ready reference, I thought you should know that I have just completed contract negotiations with a music composer, Sir Lancelot Bourguine. When he is in Europe, he has an office in Paris; he is very famous.

The contract calls for him to write the lyrics to "How to Get to Branson in the Wintertime" and also another composition "Upon Arrival, How Do I Stay Warm Enough to Sing Old Lonesome Me."

The memo was also addressed to White House intern Monica Lewinsky, President Bill Clinton and Prosecutor Kenneth Starr.

When you start a conversation or have a meeting with John Q., you can be pretty certain it's only going to last a short time. He has little time for extraneous information.

When someone goes through the revolving door that is his office, there's someone right behind waiting to go in. And when he's looking for answers, be prepared. "Most of the time he already knows the answers to the questions he asks. He just wants to be sure you know them, too," says former senior vice president Terry Bichsel. What John Q. doesn't like are surprises. Marketing director Cheryl McGee says there's another reason John Q. asks questions. "Generally, the questions he asks are the ones that he already has an answer to. And it's likely he's carrying on a conversation with himself, but you're there as a medium."

And when it comes to details, you can be sure that his photographic memory will never fail. Killian has been the subject of such tests. "Once he called me out of the blue and asked me about the clearspan on a project we were doing. I said, 'It's about 125 feet.' Mr. Hammons said, 'Don't you think it's 128 feet, Bill?' I checked the plans the next day and he was right."

John Q. isn't hard to read. It's fairly obvious he prefers shorthand conversations. And if you're trying to sell him something or give him an update, give him pictures of projects, not words. Don't go in straight with an idea: plant seeds and let them germinate.

A Different Sort of Recognition

Forget Gen X and Gen Y, forget progressive recognition plans, forget participative management and all the new expressions to describe management in the 21st century. John Q. defies all current management practices.

He's not a traditional motivator of people, and he doesn't give a lot of direct pats on the back. Compliments tend to come to John Q.'s employees sideways or through memos that talk generally about the company's success. He seldom tells people directly that their performance is outstanding. They find out by word of mouth, when he compliments the outcome of their work. His way is to tell others about successful projects: describing how well-built a hotel is, bragging about a particularly beautiful design, boasting that the hotel came in on budget, or that the hotel's satisfaction scores are high. The employees responsible should draw their own conclusions.

"Your performance review is your profit and loss statement," says Bob Fugazi, regional vice president.

In the old days of Holiday Inn, general managers were called "innkeepers." Consultant Lonnie Funk (who ultimately spent 26 years with Hammons) was working at one of Hammons' Holiday Inn hotels as an "acting innkeeper" until a full-fledged innkeeper would be brought on board. His position in limbo lasted quite some time, until one day he began to get letters addressed to him as "innkeeper." That's how Lonnie found out he had been promoted. Eventually, Lonnie, who specialized in opening hotels, opened 21 new properties for John Q. in 16 years.

Perhaps by design, considering his team is handpicked, the people who work for John Q. like being entrepreneurs and enjoy a lot of autonomy. He gives them that. They're also a self-confident bunch, who don't need pats on the back to know they're doing their jobs well. "To me, the biggest sign of his appreciation is when my paycheck shows up every two weeks," says Bob Niehaus, regional vice president. "I've been doing this a long time; I'm not dependent on the pat on the back. I can't go to the bank and deposit it." It's a sentiment that many long-time Hammons' employees share.

Indeed, people don't go to work for John Q. for recognition. They go because they want to work for the best.

Taking Care of His Team

"When I talk to his employees," says Mark Snyder of Embassy Suites, "they know him and speak fondly of him and personally of him. Some hotels I go into and I'll ask about the head of a management company, and it's obvious to me from the way they respond that what they know about that head of the company they got out of the company newsletter. When you ask Mr. Hammons' employees about him, they'll tell you about a personal story. He shares very personally with his employees. That's another thing that binds them together."

He's a friendly guy who puts people at ease and always asks, "How are the wife and kids?"

"I've never been Harvard trained," says John Q. "I'm a country guy. I'm still down to earth. And I don't deal with high falutin' MBAs."

John Q. tries to hide his soft side, but when push comes to shove, he'll quickly come to his team's aid. Mark Gundlach came to Springfield a few years back to be district director. He evaluated how the hotel could improve guest service. He found one area that he believed needed help. Bellmen were stationed inside the lobby, which meant that arriving guests didn't get assistance with their luggage until they were already inside the hotel. Gundlach moved the bell stand outdoors, where the bellmen could see and assist guests from their cars.

Because he came to the hotel for lunch each day, John Q. was well aware when the bellmen's position changed. Maybe his time in the -79 degrees in Alaska made John especially sensitive to what it feels like to be cold. Or maybe it was just his rabbit-trapping days in Fairview. In any case, he went to Gundlach and said, "Mark, what are our bellmen doing outside?" Mark explained his reasoning about improving guest service. John Q. said, "Yes, but I'm concerned about those men being outside in the cold."

"I had to reassure him that if it got too cold, I would bring them inside," says Gundlach.

At the celebration of his 80th birthday, he spoke, and in the midst became quite emotional and had to back off. It seems that, like Patton, he doesn't want anyone to see what he considers a flaw, a soft side. The reality was, he probably endeared more people to himself that day because they got a glimpse inside of him, rather than the tough, shrewd type of person he tries to show.

The people at John Q. Hammons also have something in common: a sense of humor. It's probably a necessity, considering how hard John Q. works. But it's also something he supports, because he's a big kidder himself. He loves a joke and a good story, and he's got a quick wit that he enjoys using.

Once, when Hammons was in the middle of a verbal jousting match with a banker, Jan, his executive assistant, walked into his office. She was carrying an Oh Henry! candy bar. For quite some time she listened to John Q. argue with the banker, his friend, C. C. "Coach" Fletcher, and then she finally looked at him, held up the candy bar, pointed to it and said, "Oh Henry! " He began to laugh, she began to laugh and when the laughter got totally out of control, Hammons was forced to hang up in the middle of the conversation. To this day, when she thinks he's taking things too seriously, including himself, she says to him, "Oh Henry."

Regional vice president Bob Niehaus says Hammons once turned a joke around on him. Speaking at an event, Niehaus said, "I've been with John Q. 25 years, and I like to consider myself the son he never had." John Q. came to the podium and said, "Bob, I always considered you the son I never wanted!"

Groundhog Day: His Favorite Holiday

John Q. doesn't believe in vacations, for himself or for those who work for him. In fact, his favorite holiday is Groundhog Day, because no one takes off.

To be an employee of John Q. Hammons is to know the meaning of late-night and weekend phone calls from John Q. Steve Minton, his architect gets those all the time, even though he has lunch with John Q. just about every day.

"HIS FAVORITE HOLIDAY IS GROUNDHOG DAY
BECAUSE NO ONE TAKES OFF."

On a Sunday night, John Q. might call a hotel and ask to speak to the night auditor. He's checking up on occupancy. The next day, he might call a friend to impress them with his grasp of the details of his business. He'll say, "Do you know what my occupancy was last night in Richardson?" and then tell them precisely what it was. It supports his philosophy of minding the store. The general manager at the Springfield Residence Inn says he suspects that when John Q. asks what occupancy is, he already knows the answer.

It's Old-Fashioned, But Does It Work?

How is he as a leader? A few Thanksgivings ago, everyone in the John Q. Hammons corporate office anonymously wrote down a positive description of each person in the office. The lists were collected and compiled, and each person was presented with a list of the nice things their coworkeres had said about them.

The list for John Q. speaks for his leadership style.

Here are the words his team used to describe him:
"Visionary (repeated several times on the list); loves his staff; the boss; powerful; teacher and leader; legend; gutsy visionary; brilliant; a heart of gold and a head full of new ideas; loves to develop; interesting; powerful; distinguished and inspiring; a paternal soul (whether he admits it or not); nice smile; admirable; charitable; a good leader; professional; friendly; dedicated; sharp business sense; wonderful skills of spotting trends and capitalizing on them; strong driving passion and love to develop and build architectural structures for people to enjoy and experience."

And while John Q. never did quite understand the premise behind this whole exercise, he asked Jan to be sure to save his list.

You may not agree with his methods, but you can't argue with his success, because not only did John Q. pick them, his employees picked him. And they keep picking him every day they stay at the company.

8

A Lifetime Good Sport

John Q. Hammons loves a dramatic story, and in 2001, he made one happen.

On March 1, in the Hammons Student Center, SMSU's field house in Springfield, Missouri, the crowd was primed for a great game. The SMSU Lady Bears basketball team was playing Creighton. More important, SMSU star player Jackie Stiles was likely to break the NCAA women's all-time scoring record.

In the stands, perhaps the only person as excited as Jackie was John Q. Hammons: He had a surprise for everyone.

"I had a pretty good idea of when Jackie was going to break the record, which had been 3,123. She was averaging 30-35 points a night—I've seen her score 56—and I picked that Thursday night as when I thought she would go over the top," says John.

On the Tuesday just before the Thursday game, John Q. was having a board meeting in Charlotte. While everyone else went to lunch, John Q. went—where else—to the pay phone. He started tracking down a woman named Patricia Hoskins. That name was little known to many except perhaps John Q. For the past 12 years, she had held the NCAA record. She's the one Jackie Stiles was trying to catch.

It wasn't easy to find Patricia. John Q. knew she was living in Mississippi and had attended Delta State University. But as hard as it was to track her down, true to his nature, he persisted and eventually found her. He called her at around 11 a.m. She was sleeping after working the night shift in a ceiling tile factory.

"I had a hard time trying to get her awake and tell her who I was, but I kept talking and said, 'Have you heard of Jackie Stiles?' She said, 'Yes, but I don't know her. I've seen her on TV a couple of times, but I've never seen her play.' I said, 'She's going to break your record Thursday night. I want to invite you to be there.' I said, 'All you have to do is take an hour and a half drive over to Jackson (Mississippi) and get on a TWA flight to St. Louis and then into Springfield. (I checked on all this myself.) I'll have a nice hotel room for you, and we'll escort you over to the game and you'll have a great seat. Then, after Jackie breaks your record, you can meet her. But we must make it a surprise that you're there.'"

Patricia wanted to know if she could bring her little boy. "I knew her ticket would cost $1,200, so I asked her, 'How old is your son?' She said, '12.' I said, 'How tall is he?' thinking that maybe he could get a half-price ticket. She said, 'Six foot one.' Well, that was that. I said, 'Okay, you can bring your little boy.'

"That's a true story," he says, laughing.

Patricia Hoskins did attend the game, and Jackie Stiles did break the record. After the two teams warmed up, the announcer told the crowd that the former record holder was attending. When it was all over, the two women hugged and shared a moment of glory. "It was a spine-tingling affair. I stayed the whole game," says John Q., and anyone who knows him knows just how much it means for him to sit still for an entire game.

There's no doubt John Q. admires Jackie Stiles' talent, but he also admires her spirit and her attitude. When he talks about her, he becomes even more animated than usual, and it's clear he wants everyone to know, as he does, that she's a star.

Equally important, he loves what she's done for SMSU basketball. "When she came aboard, attendance was at 3,000 a game. After she came, they filled up, with 7,000 to 9,000 people all the time."

Now You Can't Tell Anybody This...

The story of Jackie Stiles' record-breaking game is clearly his favorite story. And when he's done telling it, he always finishes with his classic line: "Now you can't tell anybody this...." Acting like he's sharing a "secret" is his way of taking people into his confidence and letting them know that what he's about to say is special. The particular "secret" about Jackie was that she would be inducted as a Missouri Sports Hall of Fame legend.

He's especially proud that Jackie has taken her place beside "legends" like Payne Stewart at the sculpture gallery outside the museum. "You know those bronze statues outside the museum? Well, I'm gonna have one put there for Jackie. You know what those things cost? $85,000. That's right. But she deserves it."

As a result of his support of Jackie Stiles, and her stellar moment with Patricia Hoskins, people wrote letters to John Q.—hundreds of letters. And they called. The first person to call told him, "You don't know me, and I don't know you. I live a hundred miles from Springfield. What you did made a 53-year-old man cry."

You didn't have to be at the game to suspect that it made an 82-year-old man cry as well.

Following sports is really John Q.'s only hobby. He appreciates a dedicated athlete, and he admires the traits that lead to excellence in any endeavor: commitment, hard work, perseverance.

Training with the Cincinnati Reds

You couldn't ask for a more loyal fan than John Q. Every year you can count on seeing him in Tampa, Florida, where the Cincinnati Reds hold their training camp. John Q. has been going for 43 straight years. He simply loves the game. And, of course, it doesn't hurt that Florida is a good place for him to work on his tan. Friend Bill Hickman, who goes with John Q. and a couple of his long time friends, says give John Q. a home plate seat in the Florida sunshine, a hot dog and a coke and he's a happy man.

When John Q. started going to the games, all those years ago, he joined a group of fans that included his friend, C. C. Fletcher and Fletcher's associate, Dan Meyer. "They were bankers, and I was

---

"THEY WOULD GET THE TICKETS, AND THEN I WOULD SERVE THE BEER AND PEANUTS."

---

trying to borrow money all the time. They would get the tickets, and then I would serve the beer and peanuts. C. C. would never drink because he didn't want to gain weight, but he'd give those peanuts hell about the third inning."

C. C. is gone now. Dan is still hanging in there. And John Q. still shows up every year for camp, although getting him to commit to a date is tough. He doesn't like to be boxed in, always preferring to keep his options open. After all, you never know when a hot deal might surface. Nevertheless, it's about the only thing that will take him away from business. Hickman says John Q. will borrow his cell phone at times, calling a friend and saying, "Do you know where I am? I'm sitting behind home plate in Florida."

At one game, John Q. actually tried to link business with the sport. He and Kemmons Wilson sat together at the World Series. John Q. saw an opportunity. "We sat right behind home plate. We'd put a dollar on every pitch—not on the pitch, but on whether the batter would get a hit or get out. Kemmons had more money than I did, and he called the pitch. I thought I'd get another franchise out of it, so I kept betting. At the end of the game, I forget who was ahead, but it was quite a deal."

The NCAA Final Four is another John Q. must, and he's been to that series for the past 37 years. If anything, he is loyal to the end.

Highland Springs Country Club

There's an excellent chance that John Q. Hammons has never played a round of golf in his life. His associate, Erik Kamfjord at Winegardner and Hammons, says, "He doesn't know a putter from a driver." But when John Q. sees a void, he has to fill it, and in his quest to create world-class opportunities for Springfield's citizens, he recognized a need for a first-class country club and a top-ranked golf course.

In 1988 he called contractor Bill Killian with a plan for developing Highland Springs Country Club. And, needless to say, when he decided to build a golf course, he wanted the best. He called the Robert Trent Jones II organization. The preeminent designer of golf courses, the Jones group has laid out some 200 courses in 38 countries on six continents, including the gorgeous panoramic course at Pebble Beach, California. Clearly, the designer and John Q. have the same desire for a great view.

As a result, Highland Springs is an award-winning, 675-acre, par 72 course that takes advantage of its position in the beautiful rolling hills of Springfield. It was nearly 40 years between the time John Q. bought six farms in southeast Springfield, and the time they became Highland Springs.

Under the auspices of the John Q. Hammons Foundation, the

course is host to the annual Price Cutter Charity Championship of the PGA Tour's Nationwide Series (formerly Ben Hogan, Nike and Buy.Com Tours). Over a dozen years, the tournament has generated more than $3 million to benefit Ozarks charities, all of which serve children.

World Golf Village

Another golf endeavor that John Q. has been associated with is World Golf Village, in St. Augustine, Florida, home of the PGA's World Golf Hall of Fame. Developers of the golf village approached John Q. to get involved in a $42-million hotel and convention center at the resort development. As usual, John Q. would build the hotel, St. Johns County would pay for the convention center and John Q. would manage it.

Missouri Sports Hall of Fame

When John Q. was finished building Highland Springs, he had a little land left over. What to do?

Cut to the Missouri Sports Hall of Fame, a not-for-profit that for 15 years had been languishing in an office basement in Jefferson City. The state assembly appropriated money to build a new Secretary of State's building in Jefferson City, about two blocks west of the capitol, and set aside a room in that building for the hall of fame. Since the room was literally a meeting room for the Secretary of State, at any given time it might be in use for things other than sports...perhaps political sports, but not the traditional ones.

Finally in 1990, Coach Norm Stewart from the University of Missouri, along with Bob Vanatta, Billy Key, and Gary Filbert, approached Hammons about refurbishing a gym on the campus in Columbia. The gym had been built in 1920; they would donate it. Not exactly the caliber of facility likely to turn Hammons on. Besides, it was going to cost as much to renovate as it would to build a new facility. The decision was easy for a development kind of guy: build a new building.

At this point, everybody got in the act. Cities across the state, from St. Louis to Kansas City, Jefferson City to Columbia, all jockeyed for position. "Put it here," they cried. But there was an ideal location for the facility, right there on that leftover land at Highland Springs. As John Q. would imagine, why not put a world-class hall of fame in front of a world-class golf course? In addition, sports are huge in southwest Missouri. Sixty-seven million visitors travel to Branson and Springfield's Bass Pro, a sporting megastore, is the state's number one tourist attraction.

Originally, the idea was for a basketball hall of fame. But John Q. saw beyond that. He determined that it would be a Sports Hall of Fame, paying tribute to the many outstanding athletes in Missouri history. He donated the land and building.

"HE IS TRULY ONE OF THE MISSOURI SPORTS LEGENDS BECAUSE OF WHAT HE'S DONE FOR SPORTS IN THE STATE."

Today, the Missouri Sports Hall of Fame stands at the entrance to Highland Springs and welcomes thousands and thousands of visitors a year. Outside, there are bronze statues of the Missouri Sports Legends, including golf legend Payne Stewart, who actually was born in one of John Q.'s Village Garden apartments; Kansas City Chiefs quarterback Len Dawson; baseball great Stan Musial; Cardinal broadcaster the late Jack Buck; Don Faurot; and SMSU basketball star Jackie Stiles. And, most notably, John Q. Hammons, inducted in 2002.

Referring to John Q.'s induction, Jerald Andrews, president and executive director of the Missouri Sports Hall of Fame said, "He's being recognized because he truly is one of the Missouri sports legends because of what he's done for sports in the state."

The 22,000-square-foot facility has museum space, a 117-seat auditorium and a gift shop. The building also houses the John Q. Hammons Library, which looks a great deal like a sports museum. There you can find autographed baseballs, bats, footballs, trophies, awards, a sports announcer's microphone and assorted accoutrements to a variety of sports. And you can also find a host of John Q. memorabilia, another "good sport."

John Q. Hammons Day

On February 10, 1996, John Q. Hammons arose knowing it was going to be his lucky day...literally. At halftime of the Missouri-Kansas game, the late Governor Mel Carnahan gave John Q. a proclamation that it was indeed John Q. Hammons Day in Missouri. Coach Norm Stewart, head basketball coach at the University of Missouri-Columbia, and Glen McDonald, president of the Missouri Basketball Coaches Association, presented John Q. with a plaque recognizing his contributions to sports. John Q. might not manage to dunk many balls in this day and age, but he certainly stands tall among sports fans.

9

Charity Begins at Home

April 13-20, 1998, was officially John Q. Hammons Week in Springfield. Mayor Lee Gannaway officiated at a ceremony in John Q.'s honor. "I didn't know if it was appropriate to give a key to the city to the man who built the city, who owns the city," said the mayor.

Several years before that ceremony, they had officially changed the name of Sherman Parkway to John Q. Hammons Parkway. (John Q. himself has named almost 90 streets in Springfield...but not this one.)

If you add up the things Hammons has contributed to the city, "giving" him a week or naming a street after him is small reward. Start with the hundreds of jobs he provides at his company's headquarters, at Highland Springs Country Club, at the Cafe restaurant and at the hotels he owns throughout the city. Those add up to the Courtyard by Marriott, Residence Inn by Marriott, University Plaza and Holiday Inn-North. Close to 300 people work

> "IF YOU'RE ABLE TO SUCCEED MONETARILY
> IN LIFE, YOU SHOULD SHARE, AND
> THAT'S WHAT I'VE DONE."

at The Chateau on the Lake alone. That itself is quite a contribution to the economy. But then add to that his charitable contributions, the list of which is almost endless. That's another investment that totals more than $50 million...that we know of.

In an article in the *Springfield Business Journal,* John Q. told reporter Kris Ann Hegle, "The city of Springfield afforded me the opportunity to get ahead. If you're able to succeed monetarily in life, you should share, and that's what I've done."

When Bob Hope suggested they rename the city "Hammonsville," he might have gotten his idea from seeing the Hammons Heart Institute at St. John's Regional Health Center (and Hammons Life Line emergency helicopter), or driving down John Q. Hammons Parkway and passing the 22-story Hammons Tower, the bronze statue of John Q. on the corner, the John Q. Hammons Building, as well as the Hammons Enterprise Center on his way to the Hammons Fountains, Hammons House Dormitories and the Juanita K. Hammons Hall for the Performing Arts at Southwest Missouri State University, or seeing a basketball game at the school's field house—also named for Hammons. Then, of course, there is the Hammons School of Architecture at Drury University, the Hammons Fountains at the Ozarks Technical Community College, and, last, but certainly not least, Hope could have visited the John Q. Hammons Library at the Missouri Sports Hall of Fame (founded by John Q.). If Bob came back in 2004 or 2005, he might see an exposition center, an 8,000-seat baseball stadium, and, oh, maybe, a hockey arena.

The fact that John Q.'s name is on so many things may not indicate so much of his desire to be edified as it does the power of his name. He says he's only put his name on three things in Springfield. The other tributes are a result of people and institutions trying to recognize his generosity. And, after all, it's good business: If you headed up a charitable group, you'd certainly want John Q.'s name on your facilities; it *is* a pretty big draw to other potential sponsors. And one thing's for sure: When John Q. and Mrs. Hammons show up at a fund-raiser, you can bet that a lot of people will turn out just to see the man and woman who are at the heart of so many things in the best interest of Springfield.

Springfield Grows Up

Use Springfield as a sample of the kind of city John Q. likes: one with potential. The metropolitan area of Springfield doubled in the years between 1970 and 2000. Some of the credit for that has to go to John Q., who has supported the city financially, developmentally, charitably and personally for 60 years.

"I came here 50 years ago when the population sign was 66,000 and Glenstone was a two-lane road. Springfield has had phenomenal growth."

He saw the growth potential Springfield had back in the '40s, and he did everything he could to make it happen. Take University Plaza as an example.

Revitalizing the City

Sometimes John Q. sees visions of where a trend is headed. Sometimes he creates a trend. That's the case at University Plaza, a down-and-out downtown area that John Q. almost single-handedly revitalized.

Because John Q. likes a panorama, if he doesn't have one handy, he'll create one. That's what he's done around his offices at the John Q. Hammons Building. He built the office in 1982 and located his own office at the top of the building. There was little to look at back then.

In 1980, he announced plans to develop a good deal of the area around the Hammons building, starting with a 270-room hotel. The only difficulty was that the deal had a Catch-22: In order to buy and clear the land, the city needed money. The banks wouldn't give them money until they owned and cleared the land. When things stalled, John Q. stepped in with his checkbook. To move things along, his University Plaza Redevelopment Corporation loaned $4 million to the city's Land Clearance for Redevelopment Authority. John Q. would be repaid with a $3.8 million federal grant from the Department of Housing and Urban Development.

In 1983, he finally opened the University Plaza Hotel, complete with his signature atrium and waterfall. In addition to its guest rooms, the hotel offers more than 24,000 square feet of meeting space.

Across the street, Hammons acquired property formerly owned by Sears-Roebuck and built the University Plaza Trade Center and exhibition hall with 69,000 square feet of meeting space.

Then, in 1988, he followed up with the Hammons Tower, the

"A LOT OF PEOPLE OWE ECONOMIC PROSPERITY TO JOHN Q. HAMMONS."

---

tallest building in Springfield (and the tallest building above sea level in the state of Missouri), which houses offices. Atop the 22-story Hammons Tower is an upscale private club.

Meanwhile, Hammons was working on developing the new United States Courthouse, which also opened in 1988.

Combined, the office, hotel and tower took care of three corners on John Q. Hammons Parkway. Yet to come was the John Q. Hammons Enterprise Center which houses the Chamber of Commerce.

The Chamber of Commerce

According to Jim Anderson, president of the Chamber of Commerce, "I don't think John Q. gets his jollies seeing his name on buildings. It goes back to John's very modest beginnings. Having his name there is not to edify Hammons or his wife as much as it is to serve as testimony to American free enterprise and the entrepreneurial spirit. I believe that his satisfaction comes not from the John Q. Hammons name, but from what it symbolizes."

The Springfield Chamber, housed in the John Q. Hammons Enterprise Center, is a success story Anderson likes to tell. "We had outgrown our office space and had been offered some free ground south of Springfield, but I wanted to stay center city. John Q. had this corner forever. The plan was that he was going to do commercial development there, which makes sense; it's a helluva corner.

"I had other ideas. I know that he likes fountains, so I had an architect friend do a little artist's rendering of what a facility might look like, including a fountain. I went to a meeting with Mr. Hammons, and I brought that with me. We were up there meeting on something else, we did our business and I said, 'Mr. Hammons, I want to share a dream with you.' He said, 'What's that?' We went over and looked down at that corner."

Jim outlined his proposition for putting the Chamber building there. As a result, Hammons gave them the ground, paid the architectural fees, and gave them a challenge grant. In all, the donation was worth almost a million dollars. "Without him capturing that vision, we could never have done this."

"A lot of people owe economic prosperity to John Q. Hammons," says Anderson.

The Future of University Plaza

That's not all Hammons has in mind for University Plaza. His panorama isn't complete. It still needs a little something recreational. Next is the $14-million Springfield Exposition Center and a AA baseball field, along with a new six-story hotel and an 80-room addition to his existing Unversity Plaza Hotel.

He's actually been working on this deal for several years—perhaps his patience is wearing thin as he follows this one last dream for the Springfield skyline. But within two years, he hopes it will be complete.

He used his typical development approach—the city has bought the land and will lease it to John Q. for $1 a year for 30 years, with an option to purchase at a nominal price. The city will help by issuing municipal bonds guaranteed and paid by John Q. Hammons (John Q.'s favorite: other people's money).

His goal is to have the $20-million stadium finished in time for the 2004 baseball season. Best of all, he wants to get a Double A minor league baseball team. "I can't tell you which team. That's a secret." Chances are, when the stadium opens, Stan Musial will be a celebrated guest. Musial once played on a class C team in Springfield before achieving legend status in the majors. As a legend of the Missouri Sports Hall of Fame, he is a friend of John Q.

Two renderings of the stadium rest against the wall in Hammons' office. John Q.'s take on the naming process is simple. He plans to

"IF THE PROJECT IS
FORWARD-LOOKING, I'M FOR IT."

call the new baseball venue Hammons Field. When someone said, "Why are you naming it after yourself?" John Q. replied, "If you've got $25 million, I'll put your name on it 25 times. "That's his sense of humor coming into play, but it also speaks to the fact that Hammons is, indeed, the one who will have to come up with the money, and it's his name that sells. Below the surface, however, you might suspect this is the culmination of his years of investment in the sport, and perhaps his lifetime dream.

At this point, John Q. can look out his window and envision the finished product. In the end, John Q. will be surrounded by those things he loves: education, at SMSU, Drury and Ozarks Technical Community College; basketball, at the SMSU field house; baseball, at the new stadium; and a couple of hotels. It's just the way he likes it.

Has the downtown reinvestment been a financial success for John Q.? Perhaps. But mostly, it has been a success for the city.

"If the project is forward-looking, I'm for it. I've enjoyed living here, and I enjoy helping."

Dr. Marshall Gordon, former president of Southwest Missouri State University, says his experience has been that most people who create wealth like to hold onto it for a significant period of time, perhaps never releasing some or all of their earnings. "We all know a lot about the charitable contributions he's made in Springfield, but he's actually done so much more through the really unknown philanthropy; the business projects he's done that he knew were not justified based solely on the numbers."

Not everyone appreciates the magnitude of John Q. Hammons' exposure in Springfield. Critics may say that he is self-aggrandizing or, perhaps, has a big ego. Mickey Powell, who lived in Springfield while working for John Q., but has also lived in a variety of other places, says, "To have an individual like Hammons is a gift. I've lived in Topeka, Dallas, Memphis, and now Batesville, Arkansas. I've never lived anywhere where you had an individual that contributed as much to the community as John Q. has to Springfield, Missouri. The hospitals, the colleges, the universities. Just the entire community. Every morning when someone in Springfield gets out of bed, they ought to give thanks that they've got a John Q. Hammons up there."

Education First

There can be no doubt that John Q. Hammons believes in education. Not only did he invest two years of his life as an educator— and he now builds his hotels near universities—he also continues to invest in the academic lives of young people in Springfield.

Dr. Gordon says, "I think the reason he's partial to education is that's how he got started. He was a school teacher and a coach. Doors were opened because of his educational experiences."

"He loves to see kids set goals," says Jan Robbins. "He will ask them, 'How smart are you? And 'Do you study hard?' That comes from his school teaching days."

Hammons received an Honorary Doctorate of Law degree in 1993 from Northwood University, and in 1987 he picked up an honorary doctorate from Drury College (now Drury University).

Northwood University

In 1957, the Soviet Union launched Sputnik I, the world's first artificial satellite. The Space Age had officially begun. According to Dr. Arthur E. Turner, that was a turning point in education as many schools diverted funds away from business classes and into science. Dr. Turner believed strongly in the need for a substantial business curriculum and ethic. With about $65,000 borrowed from his father-in-law, and the assistance of his friend R. Gary Stauffer, in 1959 Dr. Turner founded Northwood University, a school dedicated to the enrichment of students in free enterprise.

By 1988, Northwood had three campuses: Michigan, Texas and Florida. One of its distinguished "graduates" was John Q. Hammons who received an honorary Doctor of Laws degree. The school had also developed a program to recognize Outstanding Business Leaders, and in 1988 John Q. Hammons was inducted.

Since they met, Dr. Turner and John Q. have become great friends, talking on the phone every Sunday about the stock market, hotels, education, politics. "Of all the people we've honored, he is one of the outstanding ones. He knows so much about everything. Imagine how many college presidents would benefit from having a relationship with such a successful business leader. I don't believe there's another relationship like ours in the country."

As he learned of the school's mission, John Q. became so enamored of Northwood and its philosophy of getting young men and women ready for work that he has become a staunch supporter of the school. He founded the Arthur E. Turner Entrepreneur of the Year program on the Florida campus, with the purpose of bringing to the school business leaders under 40. In addition, he underwrites scholarships and occasionally lectures at the school.

Drury University School of Architecture

One day in 1984, Dr. John Moore, president of Drury University, and John Q. were discussing the future of the 118-year-old university. Dr. Moore suggested that John Q. might want to give the school a helping hand. That would make sense: Architecture is surely one of the most important elements of John Q.'s life. As they talked, John Q. took out a marker and a napkin, and sketched a proposal to give the school $2.5 million. The deal was struck, and Hammons gave a call to Killian Construction. John Q. had known Bill's grandfather and father. In fact, when Bill was 16 years old, he had made pocket money brush-hogging John Q.'s land.

"HE BELIEVES THAT BOTH SIDES SHOULD GET A WINNING DEAL."

Bill and Steve Minton (Hammons' architect) went to John Q.'s restaurant in University Plaza to have lunch with Hammons. The boss had a sketch mapping out Drury University School of Architecture. Hammons told Killian he was giving $2.5 million. Could the school be built for that? Killian agreed.

When it was complete, the school gave Drury what some people described as "a new front door." Oh, there was just one little hitch. There is (of course) a fountain in front of the school. When it was first built, Hammons didn't like it. In his down-home manner he told Killian it looked, "like a little boy wee-weeing." Once the fountain was revamped, Hammons was happy.

Killian values his relationship with John Q. "Even when he's been cutting a deal with me, he's always been watching out for my best interest. He believes that both sides should get a winning deal. Because I've built hotels for him in other locations, he's given me opportunities I wouldn't normally have had in Springfield."

The Hammons School of Architecture is in full swing now, an accredited five-year professional program offering a Bachelor of Architecture degree.

Ozarks Technical Community College

Since 1990, Springfield has been home to Ozarks Technical Community College, the largest and fastest-growing community college in the United States. The school has an open-admission, two-year program and allows students to earn one-year certificates or associate degrees.

Considering the school's focus on quality, it's no surprise that John Q. found a natural link with his own quality philosophy and his dedication to education. As a result, the school has a more beautiful and inviting campus, thanks to a $300,000 grant. The donation made possible construction of a pedestrian mall and an 8-foot-high waterfall at the school's permanent campus.

Southwest Missouri State University

When you leave John Q. Hammons' offices and travel south down John Q. Hammons Parkway, in just a short time you'll reach the campus of Southwest Missouri State University.

"He started contributing to SMS when people weren't contributing to public schools," says Jacquie, his personal financial advisor. "They got funding from the state, and there was little funding going on. He wanted to help them out."

John Q. jokes about the line to philanthropy being very, very, short; anyone can get into it almost any time. Needless to say,

John Q. is usually at the head of that short line, especially when it comes to education.

The Water Feature

Wander around the SMSU campus and at its center you'll discover a water feature, a clear clue that John Q. Hammons has his hand in the development of this school. Indeed, Hammons donated the fountains to create energy at the school, just as he has at so many of his hotels. But that's just the start.

Hammons Student Center

To show his support of Southwest Missouri State University, John Q., in 1976, provided the funding to build a 10,000-seat field house which would become the Hammons Student Center. The center was built for $5.5 million, and was named after Hammons because he offered $1 million to help finance maintenance, operation and debt service of the building. Today, the facility is the largest indoor facility in southwest Missouri, an arena big enough to hold historic moments like the night Jackie Stiles broke the NCAA women's scoring record. Students enjoy concerts and recreational facilities, including a swimming pool and racquetball and basketball courts.

Hammons House Dormitories

At one end of the SMSU campus, some old, dilapidated houses had been torn down. It wasn't exactly a drawing card for out-of-town students. The school board of regents wanted a campus with a significant amount of university-sponsored housing. So they went to Mr. Hammons, whose office was just down the street and who had already shown his desire to support the school.

The regents asked, "Would you help us build a residence hall?" In fact, prior to that time, on several occasions the university had tried on its own to get the money together. Hammons agreed to build a facility and lease it to the university. The university would pay him for his project cost, and then he would get the write-off. That's what happened.

Dr. Marshall Gordon, former president of SMSU, was there. "One of the conditions Hammons had with the board was that the only way he would build it is if it would be, as he described it, 'first class.' He said, 'It's going to be something that you'll be proud of and I'll be proud of.'" As was his custom, John Q. took out his yellow legal pad and began to draw a plan.

With nothing but a handshake, the university began to acquire property, and to tear down the remaining houses on the land it owned. "That's the way it got started, without even a contract," says Dr. Gordon.

"He would call me from time to time and say, 'Doc, do you know how much money I have in this project?' Of course, I didn't have any idea and he would tell me, 'You know we really need to get something in writing.' After one of those times, I told the board now you've really got to get this issue dealt with. So, the university's attorney drew up a triple-net lease document, and the board felt it favored Hammons more than the university. Then we reminded ourselves, hey it's our attorney that's drafting this!"

Pre-Hammons House, the university had dormitories and other housing facilities that had been very low cost for students, some perhaps as low as $100 per month. For the new facilities, they were planning to charge more than double that fee. The university officials couldn't be sure they could rent such top-line housing, but Hammons was certain they could. He was accustomed to speculating about what a market would bear, and he figured parents of students from St. Louis and Kansas City who attended SMSU would be happy to pay. He also believed the university could attract even higher quality students if they had something more appealing than a rental house to offer. He knew if he built it, they would come. It wouldn't be just another dormitory. It would be something special.

One of the features of the dorm was that each room/suite had a computer that was linked to the university's mainframe, allowing students to access the library and other offices from their rooms. Says Dr. Gordon, "If you knew how to do it, you could even change your grades! We didn't worry too much about that. We felt if the students were that smart, we'd just give 'em the grade!

"We used that residence hall to attract some quality scholars," says Dr. Gordon. "We lead the state and a number of states in national merit scholars, for example. The key to it is that we could get them a room in this residence hall that had a computer.

The university had a sign-up for students who might be interested in living in the new residence hall. It would hold approximately 600 students. In two evenings, they signed up 600 students.

For years after it was built, the university got calls from people all over the U. S. who had heard about the first-rate residence hall and wanted to use it as a model for other dorms.

Once the university got around to working out the contract for the dorm, they realized what a success the dorm could be. And with the high occupancy they predicted, they saw that the risk was gone. They wondered if Hammons would sell the residence hall to them.

"A couple of board members and I went to see Mr. Hammons, and we said 'Will you sell it to us now that we have enough students to fill it and make a cash flow? Will you sell it to us, but only for your cost? That's all we could pay.' And he said, 'Sure, I'm just doing it to help you anyway.'"

The university later built another dorm using its own money and contractors, but with a plan that John Q.'s team drew up. "I think we paid one of his employees a small fee," says Dr. Gordon, "but nothing like what it would have been had we hired an architect."

They built a replica of Hammons House, and the facility was temporarily to be called "New Hall" until they could find a name. Eventually, the name stuck. Of course students refer to the matching buildings as "Mr. and Mrs. Hammons."

According to Dr. Gordon, "An accounting firm here in town estimated that when the university bought the residence hall, they felt they'd saved about $2 million. Plus, Hammons assumed all the risk, up front."

Was it really risky business? Maybe John Q. just saw a void and filled it. He was never in it for any kind of return. He was simply demonstrating his support of the school. Some people are suspi-

---

"THE TEACHERS ASK ME WHAT THE KIDS CAN
DO FOR MR. HAMMONS AND I SAY, WRITE
HIM LETTERS. HE WILL SIT FOR HOURS
AND READ THOSE LETTERS."

---

cious of generosity like Hammons'. This was such a case. Hammons House generated a celebrated legal inquiry on which attorney Bill Hart worked with Mr. Hammons.

"The U. S. Attorney started looking at SMSU and concluded that Mr. Hammons and the school had done something wrong, as if there were some kind of payoff. The attorney called Mr. Hammons to testify. The federal courthouse is right across the street from his office, but the newspapers were following the story and they were swarming around. So, he and I got into the car and we drove into the basement of the courthouse and he testified and then we got ready to leave the same way we came. Mr. Hammons was sitting in the back of the car, and he said, 'I'll just duck down.' I told him he didn't need to do that, that we were just fine, and that we'd drive fast out of the garage. So, we came roaring out of the garage, and I looked around, and I didn't see Mr. Hammons. He was stuck down in the back seat! And that would've been fine, but he sat up just at the last minute, and a reporter was there. The next day, newspapers were reporting that Mr. Hammons was hiding in my car. I said, 'I told you not to duck down.' He said, 'I didn't.'"(If you want it to be true, it is.)

Ultimately, the inquiry turned up nothing but Hammons' love for the school and his desire to support education. In his development business, he's not in it for the money, he's in it for the satisfaction of a project well-conceived and well-executed. So it is with his charitable donations. After all, he's still a teacher at heart.

Newspapers in Education

John Q. is a friend of education and communication, and, in fact, he's actually 50 percent owner of the Network Publishing Corporation and the *Springfield Business Journal (Illinois)*. Not surprisingly, each year, John Q. donates to the Newspapers in Education program, another way he has of helping teach the younger generation. Through that program, he makes sure students have access in their classrooms to the *Springfield News Leader* and *USA Today* newspapers.

Some of the most gratifying days he has are when he receives letters from children who have benefited from the distribution of the newspaper to schools. "The best letters he gets are from the elementary school, handwritten," says Jan, his assistant. "The teachers ask me what the kids can do for Mr. Hammons, and I say, write him letters. He will sit for hours and read those letters."

Springfield Public Schools also benefit from his Foundation Challenge Grants to benefit computer technology.

And, of course, there are the individual requests that come in that tug at Hammon's heart. Through the local Make-a-Wish Foundation, a young boy related his wish to ride in a limousine and eat a meal with Mr. Hammons at The Tower Club, the restaurant on top of the Hammons Tower. On the day scheduled, because of flight changes, Mr. Hammons was unable to join the young boy while he dined at The Tower Club. The meeting between the two did take place, however, inside the limo under the canopy of Mr. Hammons' office building. Clearly outside his comfort zone, John Q. nervously asked the young boy if he was going to die. They talked for quite awhile about the young man's favorite subjects in school and sports. After all, he was also interested in sports and had been a teacher. John Q. often reflects back to that afternoon.

Planting Seeds

While John Q. has given money outright to a vast number of causes, he also believes in "teaching people to fish." He often offers challenge grants in which an organization must raise a certain amount on its own in order to receive the gift. Another Hammons method is to match contributions made by others.

According to friends, he's made many of his contributions in order to elevate the standard of living and the culture in Springfield. He's had a chance to compare Springfield with a number of other communities and to see a number of world-class facilities. He's determined that Springfield excel as well.

The Hammons Heart Institute

When most people have a heart attack, they go to a hospital. When John Q. had a heart attack, he contributed to the establishment of a heart center as part of St. John's Regional Health Center. He didn't do it right away, but when he did, it was quite a facility.

Considering his hard-driving style, it probably came as a surprise to no one when he had a heart attack on May 1, 1960. At that time, he was only 41 years old.

According to his cardiologist, John Q. had previously suffered from "chest wall pain," a symptom that was often seen in "tense individuals." John Q. was in the process of becoming a Holiday Inn franchise owner and was pushing hard to develop hotels. Although he would probably deny it, John Q. undoubtedly was subjecting himself to a lot of stress. As a result, he had chest pain.

His physician, Dr. Glenn Turner, was the doctor who first developed the Early Warning Signs of Heart Attack now used by the American Heart Association. "Among patients who suffered chest wall pain, it was common for them to be fearful of a heart attack. I made it a practice to teach these people how to distinguish between chest wall pain and pain associated with a heart attack." His practice probably saved John Q.'s life.

The day John Q. suffered his incident, he called Dr. Turner, who commonly made house calls. "Doc, I've got the other kind today. It's in the middle of my chest," said John Q., indicating his symptoms were different than what he had experienced before. The doctor went immediately to his house. After spending three weeks in the hospital, John Q. recuperated without incident. The doctor kept him on anticoagulant medication, which at that time was an unconventional treatment. It required that John Q. have a blood test every three weeks to monitor his medication. Because of his nontraditional approach, Dr. Turner came under criticism, even attracting a national spotlight. Although John Q. was doing well, he called Dr. Turner to inquire about the validity of the criticism.

"Doc, what about this? They say this treatment's not right." Dr. Turner assured him that it was, and John Q. trusted him. Eventually, Dr. Turner's practice came to be an accepted and recommended method of treating post-heart attack patients.

John Q. continues to receive treatment with anticoagulant drugs, but has never had another incident. Dr. Turner is now retired, but every time John Q. saw him in the past, he would leave on the same note: "Doc, you saved my life. I owe my career to you."

In fact, Dr. Turner owes a few things to John Q. as well, because his patient was very grateful indeed. In 1970, 10 years after John Q. suffered the first symptoms, Dr. Turner approached him with a need for money to create an intensive care unit. John Q. funded a $100,000, six-month study to determine the feasibility of an institute that would be the first of its kind to deliver emergency health care services rather than merely doing research. The study was conducted in cooperation with St. John's Regional Health Center. Its basis was the fact that being able to treat patients within one hour—called the Golden Hour of the Heart Attack— greatly increases the chances of saving patients' lives.

While that was a key factor for people who lived close by, it was especially important for those who lived in more remote areas of the region. Quick transportation to the hospital was essential in whether they would receive care within the Golden Hour.

When the study proved the need for the center, plans were drawn up for a $5.5 million regional system incorporating education, prevention, communication, transportation, hospital care, rehabilitation and research. Again, Dr. Turner approached John Q.

"I had never asked anyone for money like this, and I was almost incapacitated with apprehension," says Turner. The response from John Q.? "You've got it, Doc."

One stipulation John Q. made in the donation was that Turner never reveal the amount of the donation. "I don't want to be talking amounts because I don't want to appear to be in competition with Lester Cox," said John Q. Cox had endowed the Cox Medical Center.

Interestingly, as the intensive care center was being designed, Dr. Turner and his associates traveled and reviewed units around the country. What they found was not conducive to patient health. In most units, there was a "mechanical jungle" of equipment, ungodly noise that prevented patients from getting the sleep they needed, communal toilets and no view of the outside. Patients had no idea what time of day it was. Dr. Turner became determined to design a facility that would take into account the psychological aspects of patient care.

At one of their design meetings, Dr. Turner told his colleagues, "If John Q. Hammons can provide highly appealing accommodations at a modest price for mainstream Americans, why can hospitals not do that also?"

John Q. gave an endowment in the form of Holiday Inn stock, and in November 1972, the center opened its doors. The design did, in fact, draw admirers and resulted in a revolution in hospital design. Dr. Turner wrote a book, which John Q. subsidized, which

"IF JOHN Q. HAMMONS CAN PROVIDE HIGHLY
APPEALING ACCOMMODATIONS AT A MODEST
PRICE FOR MAINSTREAM AMERICANS, WHY
CAN HOSPITALS NOT DO THAT ALSO?"

helped spread the word about what Turner calls the "modern hotel look" in hospital design.

When the center opened, they began seeing an average of 50 patients a week. Today, they see 2,200 patients a day.

Since then, the center has had an illustrious history. In 1989, the Missouri Health Facilities Review approved a $1.1 million request to expand the facility, adding a two-story, 11,000-square-foot addition. In January 1986, a satellite clinic in El Dorado Springs, Missouri, opened, and in 2001, the facility expanded to Branson, Missouri, and the third satellite has been scheduled to open in St. Roberts, Missouri, by year-end 2002. A huge expansion is planned for 2005.

In addition, Hammons purchased a twin-turbine rescue helicopter for $1.2 million. Named the Hammons Life Line, at the time it was one of only four rescue helicopters in Missouri. While most helicopter rescues were associated with trauma that resulted from automobile accidents, this one was dedicated to heart attack patients.

In 2002, the American Medical Group Association selected Hammons Heart Institute's Congestive Heart Failure program as one of four honorees across the nation to receive the national Acclaim Award. The program was selected because of the dramatic improvements shown in patients enrolled, and the hospital received a $10,000 grant for educational purposes.

Today, HHI offers far more than cardiac care. They treat arthritis, lung disease, weight loss and other factors that contribute to healthy hearts.

Although John Q. gave only the original gift, he continues to contribute to the program by lending his name to the organization and by making appearances at fund-raising events. He began by sharing a vision in a way that would inspire others, giving the center a leg up, and standing back and watching how it could grow. And fortunately, one person who hasn't had to be a patient at the center is John Q. Hammons.

The Fairview Community Center

Just as any famous man's small-town birthplace would, Fairview, Missouri, has always wanted Quentin (as he was known in his hometown) to come to a high school reunion. He never had time. Not, that is, until he got a letter from a friend in Visalia, California.

"She used to work at our hotel, and she wrote me and sent me a picture of a sign that said, 'Fairview, Missouri, birthplace of John Q. Hammons.' I asked her where she got it, and she said she had taken the picture herself."

That piqued his interest, so he went to the reunion. "They have a big park there, and it's a nice park with a lot of trees. I saw this old barracks that had been hauled up from Camp Crowder from the war, and they had their little meeting (reunion) in one of those little old barracks. It was awful. It was not adequate, and they didn't have the money to fix it up, and I thought, 'Boy, I'll tell you what. This is something else.' So that was a lesson to me. I thought, I can afford it, so I'll just build them a new building."

Hammons and his contractor, Bill Killian, drove over to Springfield "with a sledgehammer, some spikes and a 100-foot tape measure," says Killian.

"It was a hot August afternoon, and we sat out under this big tree, drinking iced tea, and John Q. loosened his tie and chatted with the people in town."

With the plans for the center in hand, they staked out the building. Killian says, "I'd start pacing it off, and John would point and say, 'Right there.' No doubt, when I'd measure it, he'd be right on. He just has an uncanny eye for that sort of thing."

As usual, John Q. took charge of the process early on. For such a comparatively small undertaking, he certainly didn't need a market study or complex contract negotiations. "I talked with the lawyer for the town and he said, 'You don't need any instructions from us. Just go build it.' We did that with just a handshake."

Once the building was done, John Q. slid into his mode of teaching them to fish, suggesting that they charge a small fee to anyone who used the building "so that they'd be sure to clean up." The community members put in bricks with their names on the walkway, socking away the fees to help keep the center's quality high, just like Quentin would expect.

"We spent about $350,000 on it, and I insisted that they operate it right," he said. When he goes back for his 75th reunion, it should be in tip-top shape.

Public Television

In 1974, Channel 21, a public television broadcasting facility, was looking for money. It needed to generate matching funds for a grant from the Department of Health, Education and Welfare. In stepped John Q. Hammons, with a capital founders' gift of $100,000. It was his way of supporting innovative educational techniques.

Almost 20 years later, Hammons was still in the picture, big time, with a pledge of a $250,000 matching gift.

For eight years, Hammons was a member of the national board of the Public Broadcasting System.

The Performing Arts

Mrs. Hammons has her own special interests, including the performing arts. She has supported the arts throughout her life in Springfield, and has been side-by-side with John Q. behind a number of arts-related causes. John Q. has personally seen that cultural opportunities improve the quality of life in other communities, and he wants the same thing for Springfield. Besides, culture begets growth.

Over the years, John and Juanita Hammons have helped raise close to $1 million for the Springfield Ballet, the Springfield Little Theater, the Springfield Regional Opera and the Springfield Symphony.

One of the more high-profile events in which Mrs. Hammons has participated actively is the Annual Salute to the Performing Arts, a dinner she and Mr. Hammons used to host each year. John Q. would match the funds raised through the dinner.

In 1992, Hammons made a special contribution to create a 95,000-square-foot, 2,220-seat theater that would feature top-notch facilities for performances. Owned and operated by Southwest Missouri State University, the theater was built to serve the student population.

"HE WAS LIKE A MOVIE STAR WALKING DOWN THE RED CARPET."

The Board of Regents named the facility the Juanita K. Hammons Hall for the Performing Arts to honor her as not only the chairman of the private funding campaign for the theater, but as a lifelong supporter of the arts. Mrs. Hammons says her dream is to "listen to the New York Philharmonic in the Hammons Performing Arts Center."

John Q. felt that it would be a true tribute to her to name the center for her as long as its quality would represent Mrs. Hammons with the level of respect she deserves. "She is a first-class lady," says John Q., "and she deserves this."

Communities Across the Nation

According to Lou Weckstein, president, John Q. Hammon Hotels, wherever John Q. has a hotel, you can bet he's already contributed

---

"HE HAS A GIANT HEART, BUT HE'S NEVER LEARNED HOW TO MANAGE IT."

---

to the community. John Q. always wants to be sure his development benefits the community—in jobs, visitors and economic development. When he negotiates with mayors and other city representatives, he's always teaching them how they can solve their problems, look at resources they hadn't considered before or take advantage of opportunities.

Besides his capital investments in cities, however, there are other, more personal investments John Q. makes.

The city of Fort Collins, Colorado, was devastated in 1997 by a monstrous flood. John Q.'s hotel was unharmed because it had been built above the flood plain. The large majority of the citizens, however, lost some or all of their life possessions. John Q. wrote a check for $1,000 to every hotel team member who had been with him more than a year.

The Unsung Stories

In the last couple of years, Mrs. Hammons has socialized less than in their early days together. But on one occasion, she had come to the University Plaza across the street from John Q.'s office...that's the hotel where Hammons always has lunch. "She hadn't been to the property for quite some time," says District Director Mark Gundlach. "When Mr. Hammons came in for lunch, I told him Mrs. Hammons was here, and he said, 'Let's walk over.' He walked into the luncheon and was suddenly surrounded by about 15 very classy women, and he was kissing their hands and getting his picture taken with them. Basically he was like a movie star walking down a red carpet."

Not all of John Q.'s generosity makes headlines like a new university dormitory or a performing arts center. Given his prominence, he receives hundreds of requests each year for contributions large and small. He appreciates thank-yous in writing, but seems to feel uncomfortable with one-on-one encounters with those he's helped. The fact is, John Q. has a hard time saying "no," and he hesitates to open the door to even more requests.

Few people know of his expressions of heartfelt interest or involvement, but for those who do, the meaning is great. "He has a giant heart, but he's never learned to manage it," says one friend.

Says his friend, Frank Farmer, "I've known a lot of big people, but none as big as John Q."

10

A Lifetime of Achievements

"History repeats itself and I know that. You take advantage of what's happened in the past, but I always think about the future, not yesterday. I can't change the past. I can change the future."

In a lifespan of 83 active years, there are a lot of yesterdays. And if you're John Q. Hammons, the accolades add up. In fact, they add up to a whole library, The John Q. Hammons Library, housed at the Missouri Sports Hall of Fame.

Over a period of a year, close friend and project manager Marty McGahan assembled the collection of Hammons memorabilia, designing the room and sorting through 40 years worth of trophies, newspaper stories, photographs, plans, mementos, papers and other items that signify a life spent in making things happen. The library includes John Q.'s first desk, a leather-topped, crescent-shaped desk that he took in trade for a residential lot in Southern Hills. The covers of trade magazines with his picture on them. Some of many hotel awards. And the wedding picture of John Q. and Juanita K. Hammons.

It wasn't hard to gather things for the library. Hammons may not be a widely known celebrity outside of Springfield or the hotel industry, but he's clearly someone who makes an impression. Few people who meet him forget him; he leaves his mark. As Mark

Gundlach said, people save things that John Q. writes to them. "I've saved every one of his letters," Gundlach says.

Servers in the dining room of his University Plaza Hotel have kept napkins he's drawn diagrams on. Dr. Marshall Gordon saved a yellow legal sheet of a drawing of SMSU Hammons House dorms.

His career spans hundreds of hotels, several golf courses, six shopping centers, ten residential subdivisions, IMAX theaters, a

---

"AS LONG AS JOHN Q. LIVES, HE'LL BE DOING SOMETHING MEMORABLE."

---

riverboat casino and a ranch in California. He owns land in just about every state, some of it still waiting for the right development opportunity to come along.

The library recounts some pretty phenomenal accomplishments. And the amazing thing about the library is: It's still growing. As long as John Q. lives, he will be doing something memorable. On an ordinary day, John Q. personally touches hundreds of lives, getting people excited about possibilities, giving them opportunities, helping them see what may be over the next hill.

U. S. Representative Roy Blunt, R-Bolivar, called Hammons "a friend of the arts, healthcare and sports. We wouldn't have a place to watch basketball, the health care facilities or the Hall of Fame if it wasn't for him."

In 2002, John Q's public company refinanced $510 million in debt, paving the way for a more solid future.

And John Q. plans to be a part of that future. He still has a phone near at hand, and he's getting ready to buy a jet. At his age, he says he deserves to be more comfortable. And, with security restrictions the way they are at airports, you can imagine that it does infringe a bit on his time. He wants to be free to come and go when and where he pleases, and, yeah, at 83 he probably has earned a comfortable ride.

Just Around the Corner: Retirement 2011

Dear Kemmons and Dorothy:
It's been some time since I have written to the "Mother of the year, every year," but, of course, I think of you all often. Mrs. Hammons and I are planning to go to London—I think. It's still difficult for me to create "time available." If we get to London, I sure hope we can see and visit with you both.

We are taking the liberty to enclose our new directory. In case you hadn't heard, my new retirement date is October 1, 2011, at 1:00 p.m. Somebody inquired about the "1:00 p.m." time, and I expressed that there would still be daylight by which to watch the leaves!!!!!

The date on the letter was September 8, 1992. Much has changed since then. Mrs. Wilson passed away in 2000. Mr. Wilson and Mrs. Hammons no longer travel. But John Q.'s retirement date hasn't changed. He's still going strong.

To be with Mrs. Hammons, he travels a bit less, perhaps only 3-4 days every couple of weeks. That's a switch for the office team, as well; they're on the run quite a bit more when he's in town. Despite his lighter travel schedule, though, he's still pursuing development hot and heavy.

With the Chateau now five years old, Hammons is onto some brand new babies. One is the just-opened Renaissance Hotel in Richardson, Texas, an updated Marriott prototype. Competitor Mark Snyder of Embassy Suites speaks of how John Q. has kept up. "If you think for one minute that Mr. Hammons doesn't understand the world today, you need to look at this hotel. It's very Euro/Asia, San Francisco meets Seattle. It's the most extraordinary, extravagant, funky hotel you've ever seen." Since Euro/Asian is becoming a sought after style today, it's not surprising that John Q. would be at the front of the wave. As Gundlach says, "He continues to put his feet into the shoes of the customers."

He's also looking forward to the 8,000-seat stadium that will complete his (current) vision of what Springfield needs. When that's done in 2004, he will be surrounded by the things he loves: his office, his hotel, his business enterprise center, his stadium, his universities, and his team.

"He's obviously had a good time, and he'll do it until the day he dies," says a Hammons board member, David Sullivan. "He will for sure, and he'll have a set of plans under his arm when he goes."

"IF HE'S MOVING THROUGH YOUR LIFE, HE MAKES IT BETTER."

How does John Q. see himself? His friend Frank Farmer, wrote a profile of John Q. in 1971, in which the man described himself.

"I'm an average American with perhaps more desire and drive than most people. I'm not afraid to pay the price for success that most people shrink from, and that is work. For every dollar I've made, many people beside me are making that same dollar. No contract is worth entering into unless both people want to make it work. Because of this philosophy I've had very little trouble. I am humble, appreciative and thankful for the opportunity I have to live each day in America, where the freedom and opportunity to live and to work excels that of any place in the world. We don't stop to appreciate that as much as we should."

Has he changed? Not much. He continues to put himself in the shoes of the customer. Maybe he's not quite as naive as he once was: In a life as long as his, there are always some disappointments, both business and personal. It's made him a bit more reserved with his trust.

According to those who know him well, in some ways he's mellowed. But that's not to say he's slowed down. In fact, he's a bit more driven today, because he realizes he still has much to accomplish in a limited time. After all, he only has until 2011.

"Wheel, deal, work. That's my pleasure. That's my vacation. Can I enjoy myself being idle? I don't think so; I never have. I never tried it."

Now that you know John Q. Hammons, you can draw your own conclusions about his life. One thing is for sure: The story of John Q. Hammons is one of a man who created much, who delivered what he promised, who made his mark not only on Springfield, Missouri, and on the hotel industry, but also on the thousands of people he touched in his long and eventful life.

"We will be remembered, not by the material goods we have accumulated, but by the good we have accomplished along our way, by the way we share, or have shared, or will share, the fruits of our achievement with our fellow men and our country."

He will undoubtedly be remembered by what he has shared.

Now that's a true story.

John Q. Words of Wisdom

*Circulated at the request of John Q. Hammons

The Optimist

The optimist fell twenty stories.
At each window, he shouted to his friends:
"Everything is all right so far!"

Author Unknown

"That's not my job"

This is a story about four people named Everybody, Somebody, Anybody and Nobody. There was an important job to be done and Everybody was sure that Somebody would do it. Anybody could have done it, but Nobody did it. Somebody got angry about that, because it was Everybody's job. Everybody thought Anybody could do it, but Nobody realized that Everybody wouldn't do it. It ended up that Everybody blamed Somebody when Nobody did what Anybody could have done.

Author Unknown

John Q. (left) teams up with the Holiday Inn threesome: Kemmons Wilson, Wallace Johnson and Bill Walton.

Two Sports from Springfield, MO, Roy E. Winegardner and John Q. discuss high-rise plans for Syracuse.

His favorite activity: announcing a new project.
(Wonder if the franchisor knew about this one?)

C.C. Fletcher "Coach" (second from left) was a mentor guiding John Q. through the early banking deals.

Mr. and Mrs. Claude Fletcher

An avid baseball fan, John Q. has attended
Cincinnati Reds' spring training since 1958.

A rare
moment
of leisure
pleasure
with friends.
Outings
provide
a chance
to work
on his tan.

The evolution of John Q.'s tastes in design. An early hotel in Billings, Montana...

...out west to Portland...

...to a recent development in Oklahoma City.

The Embassy Suites - Cary (Raleigh/Durham), North Carolina

Renaissance Hotel - Oklahoma City, Oklahoma

Renaissance Hotel - Richardson (Dallas) , Texas

His pride and joy: The Chateau on the Lake.

Kemmons Wilson and wife, Dorothy, who John called "Mother of the Year Every Year," attend the celebration of John Q.'s 40th year in the hotel business.

Sam Walton and John Q. at the dedication of Glass Hall at SMSU Campus (April 6, 1988)

John Q. with friend Ray Schultz (1998).

John Q. and Roy Winegardner receive the UCLA Investment Seminars Lifetime Achievement Award in 2000.

John Q. and contractor Bill Killian team up on flights around the country to scout land and work deals.

Groundbreakings are a vital part of the development process.

Checking on The Chateau construction site (1997).

Last minute revisions to a set of plans.

Getting the story first hand from the job site.

Birthday
bash.
John Q.
celebrates
80 years
in style.

Three women
in his life:
Jan Robbins,
Mrs. Hammons,
Jacquie Dowdy
(1994).

John Fulton, VP of design and a watercolor artist, gave John Q.
this collage of his accomplishments for his 80th birthday.

Former President
Bush with John Q.
and Mrs. Hammons.

John Q.
rubs shoulders
with celeb
newsman
Sam Donaldson.

Former British
Prime Minister
Margaret Thatcher
with John Q.

The Palace Theater at Broadway at the Beach,
Myrtle Beach, South Carolina.

Entertainer Kenny Rogers and the Hammonses
opening night at The Palace Theater.

The Springfield "skyline" with the University Plaza, Holiday Inn University Plaza, John Q. Hammons building and trade center (conceptualized in the early '80s).

His lunchtime retreat, University Plaza Hotel.

The Chamber's Enterprise Center land was donated by John Q.

Hammons Tower is the tallest building in the city.

Shown with a file folder under his arm, this statue stands
as a cornerstone to John Q.'s Springfield panorama.

John Q.'s latest vision: Hammons Field in
Springfield. Due to open Spring 2004, it
will complete his panorama of
downtown revitalization.

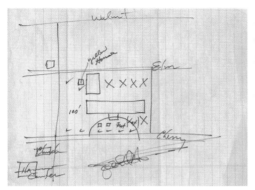

Some of John Q.'s greatest ideas start as scribbles on a yellow pad. This was the start of the dormitory project for SMSU.

John Q. and Dr. Marshall Gordon worked together on plans for SMSU campus expansions.

Hammons House dormitory helps attract high-quality students.

The campus mall was developed around the
fountain through John Q. Hammons' generosity.

John Q. Hammons Fountain at Southwest
Missouri State University Campus (1981).

Hammons Student Center at SMSU hosts Bears and Lady Bears basketball.

Jackie Stiles led the SMSU Lady Bears and broke the Women's NCAA scoring record in the Hammons Student Center fieldhouse.

Juanita's tireless dedication made
her dream come true: a performing
arts center in Springfield.

The Juanita K. Hammons
Hall of the Performing Arts.

Dr. John Moore bestows on John an
honorary degree from Drury College.

The Hammons School of Architecture located on
the campus of Drury University (1994).

Providing newspapers to youth is one way John Q. promotes education.

Northwood University (Florida campus) continues to receive John Q.'s support.

The Hammons Heart Institute nows sees
some 2000 patients a day.

The Hammons Life Line helicopter
helps save lives by getting
patients treatment quickly.

Hometown homage. John Q. wasn't aware of this sign until a friend in California told him about it.

Staking out the Community Center site.

John Q. at the dedication of the Fairview Community Center.

The Missouri Sports Hall of Fame started out as the Basketball Hall of Fame.

John Q. expanded the scope to include all sports.

Former St. Louis Cardinals' Manager Whitey Herzog.

Another sports "pro," announcer Bob Costas.

Two members of the Missouri Sports Hall of Fame: John Q. and baseball great Stan Musial.

Located in the Missouri Sports Hall of Fame,
the John Q. Hammons Library features
so many years of work.

John Q. took this original desk in trade, an
early sign of his negotiating skills.

Highland Springs Golf Course is an
award-winning Robert Trent Jones design.

The John Q.
of today.

Now that's a true story.

INDEX

THEY CALL HIM JOHN Q.

BIBLIOGRAPHY

Davis, Ron, "Portrait of a Visionary," *417 Magazine*, June, 2000.

Strainchamps, Ethel, "Citizen of the Week," *Bias Magazine*, May 2, 1951.

Wilson, Kemmons, with Robert Kerr, *Half Luck and Half Brains*, Hambleton-Hill Publishing, 1996.

Witzel, Michael Karl, *The American Motel*, MBI Publishing, 2000.

THEY CALL HIM JOHN Q.